out of joint

ROYAL COURT

Out of Joint and the Royal Court present

TALKING TO TERRORISTS

By **Robin Soans**

First performed at the Theatre Royal, Bury St Edmunds on 21 April 2005.

21-23 April

Theatre Royal, Bury St Edmunds
01284 769 505 www.theatreroyal.org

26 - 30 April

Oxford Playhouse
01865 305305 www.oxfordplayhouse.com

4 - 7 May

Malvern Theatres
01684 892277 www.malvern-theatres.co.uk

10 - 14 May

West Yorkshire Playhouse, Leeds
0113 213 7700 www.wyp.org.uk

17 - 21 May

Library Theatre, Manchester
0161 236 7110 www.librarytheatre.com

24 - 28 May

New Wolsey Theatre, Ipswich
01473 295900 www.wolseytheatre.co.uk

1 - 4 June

Warwick Arts Centre, Coventry
024 7652 4524 www.warwickartscentre.co.uk

14 - 18 June

Salisbury Playhouse
01722 320333 www.salisburyplayhouse.com

21 - 25 June

Liverpool Everyman
0151 709 4776 www.everymanplayhouse.com

From 30 June

Royal Court, London
020 7565 5000 www.royalcourttheatre.com

TALKING TO TERRORISTS

by **Robin Soans**

CAST

An ex-member of the National Resistance Army, Uganda **Nodira** **Girl** **Ingrid**	Chipo Chung
Aftab **An ex-member of the U.V.F.** **An ex-Ambassador**	Jonathan Cullen
Edward **Another ex-Secretary of State** **Michael**	Christopher Ettridge
John **A British Army Colonel** **Jad** **An ex-member of the Kurdish Workers Party**	Alexander Hanson
Momsie **An Archbishop's Envoy** **An ex-member of the I.R.A.** **Dermot**	Lloyd Hutchinson
Marjory **Rima** **Phoebe**	Catherine Russell
Faiser **The ex-head of the Al Aqsa Martyrs Brigade, Bethlehem** **Matthew**	Chris Ryman
An ex-Secretary of State **Waitress** **Linda** **Caroline** **Wife**	June Watson

Director	Max Stafford-Clark
Designer	Jonathan Fensom
Lighting Designer	Johanna Town
Sound Designer	Gareth Fry
Music Arranger	Felix Cross
Assistant Director	Naomi Jones
Casting	Amy Ball
Production Manager	Gary Beestone for Background Ltd
Company Stage Manager	Terence Eldridge
Deputy Stage Manager	Sally McKenna
Assistant Stage Manager	Lizzie Dudley
Dialect Coach	William Conacher
Costume Supervisor	Frances Gager
Associate Lighting Designer	Tim Bray / Heidi Riley
Associate Sound Designer	Angela McCluney
Set Construction	Scena Projects Ltd
Sound Hire	Cue One

For Out of Joint:

Producer	Graham Cowley
Marketing Manager	Jon Bradfield
Administration & Education Manager	Natasha Ockrent

For the Royal Court:

Production Manager	Paul Handley
Marketing	Penny Mills
Press	Ewan Thomson
Education Officer	Emily McLaughlin

Kind thanks to:
Seiko UK Ltd, and **Vision Express.**

It took a year to research, write and rehearse *Talking to Terrorists*, during which many people gave their time and expertise. Elyse Dodgson of the Royal Court and Scilla Elworthy of Peace Direct were instrumental in bringing together many of the individuals whose voices became the play's characters. Their stories were collected, in the rehearsal room and elsewhere, by a team of actor-researchers: Philip Arditti, Nathalie Armin, Chipo Chung, Sidney Cole, Matthew Dunster, Nabil Elouahabi, Lloyd Hutchinson, Naomi Jones, Kika Markham, Bella Merlin, Ian Redford and Chris Ryman. The people they met, several of whom have asked not to be named, spoke candidly and often bravely. This work would be impossible without their help and enthusiasm. We are grateful to them all.

One story we heard seemed particularly significant. A relief-worker told us of arriving at a large village which had been completely destroyed. The people there were angry not because they had nothing to eat and nowhere to live but because no-one had listened to their story of what had happened. 'A huge part of what we call terrorism arises from no-one listening,' she said.

Robin Soans and Max Stafford-Clark
April 2005

CAST

Chipo Chung

Chipo recently appeared in *The Lunatic Queen* at Riverside Studios. Other **theatre** includes *Tall Phoenix* (Belgrave, Coventry); *Ma Rainey's Black Bottom* (Liverpool Playhouse); *The Mayor of Zalamea* (Liverpool Everyman); and Ophelia in *Hamlet* (Nuffield, Southampton). **Television** work includes *Absolute Power* and she is in the **film** *Proof*. Chipo works for S.A.F.E. (Sponsored Arts for Education), a British charity supporting African actors.

Jonathan Cullen

Jonathan appeared in Out of Joint's *The Permanent Way* (OjO/National Theatre), *Feelgood* (Hampstead and West End) and *Our Country's Good* (Young Vic). Previous work at the Royal Court includes *Nightsongs, Under the Blue Sky, Our Late Night, Rafts and Dreams* and *Falkland Sound*. Other **theatre** includes: For the National Theatre, UK: *Albert Speer, Ghetto, Fuente Ovejuna, Bartholomew Fair* and *The Strangeness of Others*; *Master & Margherita, Nathan the Wise, The Seagull* (Chichester); *Goodbye Gilbert Harding* (Theatre Royal Plymouth/tour); *Grace Note* (Old Vic); *The Merchant of Venice* (Sheffield Crucible); *Desire Under the Elms* (Shared Experience); *Vieux Carre* (Nottingham Playhouse); *Morning & Evening* (Hampstead); *Miss Julie* (Salisbury Playhouse); *Venice Preserv'd* (Manchester Royal Exchange); *Dr Faustus* (Greenwich); *Chatsky* (Almeida); *'Tis Pity She's a Whore, A Woman Kill'd With Kindness* (RSC); and work at the Bush, Lyric Hammersmith and Bristol Old Vic. **Films** include *Finding Neverland*. **Television** appearances include *Midsomer Murders, Dalziel and Pascoe, Henry IV, A Woman at War*.

Christopher Ettridge

Christopher Ettridge's previous work at the Royal Court includes *About the Boy/Bluebird, One More Wasted Year, Stranger's House, Three Birds Alighting on a Field, Colquhoun and McBride* and *Some Singing Blood*. Other **theatre** includes *Democracy, Dinner* and *The Shape of the Table* (National Theatre); *Henry VI Parts 1, 2 and 3* and *Richard III* (RSC); *Dreaming* (Queen's Theatre); *Twelfth Night, A Midsummer Night's Dream, Two Gentlemen of Verona* and *Bartholomew Fair* (Regent's Park); *The Ice Chimney* (Lyric Hammersmith); *The Cherry Orchard* and *The Strongest Man in the World* (Roundhouse); *The Lady from the Sea* (Riverside Studios); *Serving it Up* (Bush); *Trumpets & Raspberries* (Phoenix); *Winter in the Morning* (Watford Palace); *Intimate Exchanges* (Bristol Old Vic); *King John's Jewel* and *Midnight at the Starlite* (Birmingham Rep); *Can't Pay, Won't Pay* (Cambridge Theatre Company); *Working Class Hero* (Nuffield, Southampton); *Joking Apart* (Crucible, Sheffield); *The Caretaker, Hamlet, Antonio* and *Toads* (Nottingham Playhouse). **Theatre directing** includes *Vassa Zheleznova* (Drama Centre); *Outside Edge* (Haymarket Basingstoke); *The Visit* (University of Eastern Connecticut); *Children of the Sea* (ALRA). **Television** includes PC Deadman in nine series of *Goodnight Sweetheart, A is for Acid, EastEnders, Bramwell, The Old Curiosity Shop, Hard Times, Casualty, Minder, Goodbye Columbus, The Bill, Love Hurts, Rag Doll, Death is Part of the Process, The Glory Boys* and *Antony and Cleopatra*. **Films** include *Origins of Evil, Julius Caesar, I Capture the Castle, Kevin and Perry, Esther, Queen of Persia, Warburg* and *The Chain*.

Alexander Hanson

Alexander played Brennen in *Shallow End* at the Royal Court. Other **theatre** includes *The Real Thing* (Royal Theatre, Northampton); *Copenhagen* (National Theatre tour); *The Villain's Opera, Troilus and Cressida, Candide, The Merchant of Venice, The London Cuckolds* (National Theatre); *We Will Rock You, The Things We Do For Love, Sunset Boulevard, Arcadia, Valentine's Day, Matador* (all West End); *Cracked, The Memory of Water* (Hampstead); *Enter the Guardsman, Brel* (Donmar Warehouse); *A Little Night Music* (Chichester Festival Theatre & West End); *The Royal Baccarat Scandal, Hay Fever, Translations, Mr Puntila and his Man Matti, A Man for All Seasons, An Ideal Husband, Game of Love and Chance, Fire Raisers, Robert and Elizabeth* (Chichester Festival Theatre); *Intimate Exchanges* (Northcott, Exeter); *Time of My Life* (national tour); *Aspects of Love* (West End and tour), *Playing with Fire* (Orange Tree, Richmond). **Television and film** includes *Kidulthood*, Marshall in *The Fugitives*, *Murder City II*, Tarquin in two series of *Auf Wiedersehn Pet, The Bill, The Last Detective II, Rosemary and Thyme, Heartbeat, Beech is Back, Relic Hunters, Casualty, The Merchant of Venice, The Escort, Unfinished Business, Peak Practice V, Doctor Finlay, Poetry Readings, Ffizz, Fellow Traveller, Museums of Madness, The Black Candle, Taking the Floor, Boon, The Chief, Six Characters in Search of an Author*. **Radio** includes *Oxygen, Amy's View, Cabaret, Gigi*.

Lloyd Hutchinson

Lloyd was in Out of Joint's *The Permanent Way*, and *Shopping and Fucking, The Break of Day* and *Three Sisters* (OjO/Royal Court). For the Royal Court he has appeared in *Some Voices* and *The Beauty Queen of Leenane* (Royal Court/Druid). Other **theatre** includes: For the RSC: *Troilus and Cressida, A Month in the Country, A Jovial Crew, The School of Night, Tamburlane the Great* part 1 & 2, *Travesties, The Art of Success, Cowboys II, The Last Days of Don Juan, Edward II, Love's Labours Lost, Curse of the Starving Class, The Pretenders, Events While Guarding the Bofors Gun; The Night Season* (National Theatre); title role in *Sherlock Holmes in Trouble, The Taming of the Shrew* (Royal Exchange); *Stones in his Pockets* (Duke of Yorks); *One for the Road* (West End/Broadway); *The Tempest, Translations* (Abbey, Dublin); *English Journeys* (Hampstead); *Playboy of the Western World* (Sheffield Crucible); *School for Wives* (Belfast Civic Arts Theatre/Dublin Festival); *Romeo and Juliet, Peer Gynt, The Merry Wives of Windsor* (National Theatre). **Film and Television includes:** Stephen Frears' forthcoming film *Mrs Henderson Presents, Pulling Moves, Gladiatress, Murphy's Law, Lloyd and Hill, Boxed, Rebel Heart, In Defence, With Or Without You, Space Island One, Inspector Morse, The Bill, London's Burning, Making News, The Nightwatch, Scout*. **Radio includes:** *Cheating the Gallows, A Wild Ride to Dublin, Pressing the Flesh, Under the Net, Measure for Measure, At Freddies, The Giant O'Brien, From a Great Height, The Faerie Queen, The Public, Unwritten Law, Vital Signs, Dubliners, The Steward of Christendom, Playboy of the Western World, The Trick of Togetherness, Baldi*.

Catherine Russell

Catherine performed in *The Break of Day* and *The Three Sisters* (Out of Joint/ Royal Court) and took part in original workshops for *The Positive Hour* (OjO/Hampstead) and *The Queen and I* (OjO/ Royal Court). Other **theatre** includes *The Day I Stood Still* (National Theatre); *A Chaste Maid in Cheapside* and *Venus and Lucrece* (Almeida); *The Way of the World*, *Arms and the Man* (Royal Exchange, Manchester); *Sailor Beware!*, *The Ghost Train* (Lyric Hammersmith); *After the Dance* (Oxford Stage Company);*The Last Carnival* (Birmingham Rep). **Film** includes *Bridget Jones: The Edge of Reason*, *Clockwork Mice*, *Solitaire for 2*, *Soft Top, Hard Shoulder* and *The Lake*. **Television** includes *Chandler and Co* (2 series), *The Cazalets (series)*, *Single* (series), *Always and Everyone* (series), *Chelworth* (series); *Holding On*, *Messiah 3*, *Waking the Dead*, *Maigret*, *The Vision Thing*, *Airbase*, *Sea of Souls*, *Silent Witness*, *Outside the Rules*, *Sherlock Homes*, *Eastenders*, *An Unsuitable Job for a Woman*, *The Bill*, *Wilderness*. **Voice** work includes *Monster* for the Scottish Chamber Orchestra, *The Servants' Room* for Radio 4 and singing in cabaret for the Theatre Museum.

Chris Ryman

Chris played Seyton/ Captain in Out of Joint's recent *Macbeth*. Other **theatre** includes Ryman in *Ryman and the Sheik*, *Probe* (Soho); *BBA & Proud* (Lyric Studio); *Confessions of a Showgirl* (Theatre Upstairs); *Foxhole* (Old Red Lion) and *Twelfth Night* (National Theatre). **Television** includes *The Bill*, *Messiah 3*, *Doctors*, *Passer By*, *2nd Generation*, *Casualty*, *The Bill* and *Alan Partridge 2*. His **films** include *Capital Punishment*, *Two Minutes* and *Iffy*. For the last two years Chris has performed, developed and improvised **comedy** characters including at Soho Theatre in *Probe* and the Edinburgh Festival. His best-known characters are Detective Inspector Patel and The Rev. Augustus Wilson. He is currently writing a comedy sketch show for television.

June Watson

June's previous work with Out of Joint includes *Our Lady of Sligo* (OjO/ National Theatre), *Sliding With Suzanne* and *Blue Heart* (OjO/Royal Court). Other Royal Court appearances include *Kosher Harry*, *Small Change*, *Beside Herself*, *Glasshouses*, *Saved*, *Over Gardens Out*, *Life Price* (Royal Court). Other **theatre** includes: *Romeo and Juliet* and *Pilate* (RSC); *Scenes from the Big Picture*, *The Good Hope*, *Cardiff East*, *The Prince's Play*, *Le Cid*, *Rutherford and Son*, *Machinal*, *Billy Liar*, *Whale*, *Garden of England*, *As I Lay Dying*, *The Beggar's Opera*, *The Long Voyage Home*, *The World Turned Upside Down*, *The Passion*, *Lark Rise*, *Sir is Winning*, *State of Revolution* (National); *The Ha Ha* (Hampstead); *Hanky Park* (Mermaid); *Waiting for the Parade* (Lyric Hammersmith); *Hippolytus* (Almeida); *Wars of the Roses*, *The Winter's Tale*, *Coriolanus* (English Shakespeare Co. UK, USA and World Tour). **Television** includes: *The Key*, *William and Mary*, *Inspector Lynley*, *Midsomer Murders*, *In a Land of Plenty*, *Common as Muck*, *A Mugs Game*, *Taking Over the Asylum*, *Five BBC Plays for Today*, *Shoot for the Sun*, *In Denial of Murder*. **Film** includes *Ghost Hunter*, *102 Dalmations*, *Highlander IV*, *The Last Yellow*, *The Knowledge*, *Bloody Kids*.

CREATIVE TEAM

William Conacher (Dialect Coach)
Previous work for Out of Joint includes *She Stoops to Conquer* and *A Laughing Matter* (with the National Theatre). At the Royal Court, *Honeymoon Suite* and *Crazyblackmuthafuckinself*. Other theatre work includes *Billy Elliot the Musical* (Victoria Palace); *The Producers* (Theatre Royal Drury Lane); *A Life in the Theatre* (Apollo); *One Flew Over the Cuckoo's Nest* (Gielgud); *World Music* (Donmar Warehouse); *The Woman Who Cooked Her Husband* (New Ambassadors); *Singer*, *The Price* and *King Hedley II* (Tricycle). William has worked extensively in regional theatre, most notably at the Royal Exchange and Library Theatres in Manchester but also at Sheffield Crucible, West Yorkshire Playhouse, Birmingham Rep, Theatr Clwyd and Chichester Festival Theatres. Television work includes Nick Dear's *Byron; Dead Gorgeous, Fallen, Hustle* and *Final Demand*. Film credits are *The Rocket Post*, *Topsy Turvy, My Kingdom, Agent Cody Banks: Destination London* and *Mr Ripley's Return*, with *Tristan and Isolde, Hooligans* and *Irish Jam* set for release in 2005. William has been dialect coach at RADA since 1998.

Graham Cowley (Producer)
Out of Joint's Producer since 1998. His long collaboration with Max Stafford-Clark began as Joint Stock Theatre Group's first General Manager for seven years in the 1970s. He was General Manager of the Royal Court for eight years, and on their behalf transferred a string of hit plays to the West End. His career has spanned the full range of theatre production, from small fringe companies to major West End shows and large scale commercial tours. Outside Out of Joint, he has most recently produced his own translation of *End of Story* at the Chelsea Theatre and is currently engaged on the 'Forgotten Voices from the Great War' project. So far there have been a season at the Pleasance Theatre and its sequel *What the Women Did* at Southwark Playhouse – more are to follow.

Felix Cross (Music Arranger)
Felix worked with Out of Joint on *Macbeth*. He has been the Artistic Director of NITRO (formerly Black Theatre Co-operative) since 1996. For NITRO: *High Heel Parrotfish* (Composer & Music Director), *Slamdunk* (book and co-director); *ICED* (director); *Passports to the Promised Land* (book, music and lyrics); *Tricksters' Payback* (music and lyrics); *Up Against The Wall* (book co-written with Paulette Randall). He has also produced four years of the annual NITRObeat festival as well as A NITRO At The Opera in partnership with the Royal Opera House. Other work includes: *Blues For Railton* (book, music and lyrics; Albany Empire); *Glory!* (book, music and lyrics; Temba/Derby Playhouse); *Mass Carib* (book, music and lyrics; Albany Empire/South Bank); *Integration Octet* (for string quartet and steel pan quartet at Aldeburgh Festival/Royal Festival Hall); *Jekyll & Hyde* and *The Bottle Imp* (both music and lyrics; books by Graham Devlin, for Major Road). He regularly composes for Radio dramas and has also written music for over fifty stage plays including the entire canon of Agatha Christie's plays (23 of them) for the Palace Theatre Westcliff. He directed *The Panbeaters* for Greenwich Theatre and has also directed plays for Radio 4.

Jonathan Fensom (Designer)
Jonathan designed *Duck* for Out of Joint and the Royal Court. Other recent **theatre** includes: *National Anthems* (Old Vic); *Twelfth Night* (West End); *Journey's End* (West End); *Cloud Nine* (Sheffield Crucible); *The Sugar Syndrome* (Royal Court); *Breakfast with Emma* (Shared Experience); *Little Baby Nothing* (Bush Theatre); *Born Bad, In Arabia We'd All Be Kings* (Hampstead Theatre); *Abigail's Party* (Hampstead Theatre, West End and UK tour); *A Small Family Business, Little Shop of Horrors* (Leeds); *My Night With Reg, Dealer's Choice* (Birmingham); *Be My Baby* (Soho Theatre Company UK tour); *After the Dance* (Oxford Stage Company); *The Mentalists* (RNT); *So Long Life* (Bath, UK tour); *Hay Fever* (Oxford Stage Company, UK tour); *Wozzeck* (Birmingham Opera, European tour); Other theatre includes: *Erpingham Camp* (Edinburgh, tour); *Alarms and Excursions* (Producciones Alejandro Romay, Argentina); *A Streetcar Named Desire, Richard III, Bouncers* (Colchester); *East* (West End, UK tour); *Wait Until Dark, The Importance of Being Earnest, Billy*

Liar, (Salisbury); *September Tide* (West End). **Television and film** includes: *tvSSFBM EHKL* (BBC Arena), *Tomorrow La Scala* (BBC films). Jonathan was Associate Designer on Disney's *The Lion King*, which premiered on Broadway and has subsequently opened worldwide.

Gareth Fry (Sound Designer)
Gareth worked with Out of Joint on *Macbeth*. For the Royal Court: *Forty Winks*, *Under the Whaleback*, *Nightsongs*, *Face to the Wall*, *Redundant*, *Mountain Language*, *Ashes to Ashes*, *The Country*. He trained at the Central School of Speech & Drama in theatre design. His work as a sound designer and occasionally as a composer includes: For Complicite: *Strange Poetry* (with the LA Philharmonic Orchestra), *Noise of Time* (with the Emerson String Quartet), *Mnemonic* (associate), *Genoa 01*. For the National Theatre, UK: *Theatre of Blood*, *Fix Up*, *Iphigenia at Aulis*, *The Three Sisters*, *Ivanov*, *The Oresteia*. For the Donmar Warehouse: *World Music*, *The Dark*. Other theatre includes: *Astronaut* (Theatre O), *Giselle* (Fabulous Beast), *By the Bog of Cats* (Wyndhams Theatre), *Blithe Spirit* (Savoy Theatre), *Zero Degrees* and *Drifting* (Unlimited Theatre), *Galileo's Daughter*, *Don Juan*, *Man & Superman* (Peter Hall 2004 season, Theatre Royal Bath), *Time* and *Space* (Living Dance Studio, Beijing), *Shape of Metal* (Abbey, Dublin), *Living Costs* (DV8 at Tate Modern), *The Watery Part of the World* (BAC), *Midsummer Nights Dream* (Regents Park Open Air Theatre), *Eccentricities of a Nightingale* (Gate, Dublin), *Mr. Placebo* (Traverse), *Forbidden Broadway* (Albery), *Holy Mothers* (New Ambassadors), *Accrington Pals* (Chichester), *Wexford Trilogy* (OSC), *Play to Win* (Yellow Earth). He also designs the music and sound system for Somerset House's ice rink.

Naomi Jones (Assistant Director)
Educated at Manchester University and Goldsmiths College, London. Directing credits include *Spring Awakening*, *Blood Wedding* and *Skylight* (Stephen Joseph Studio, Manchester) *Amadeus* (Edinburgh Fringe), *Three Sisters* (Contact Theatre) *Blue Remembered Hills* (Courtyard Theatre) and *Bloody Poetry* (Brockley Jack Theatre). For Out of Joint Naomi has worked on *Macbeth*, *The Permanent Way* and *Duck* and was Associate Director on *Sisters, Such Devoted Sisters*.

Robin Soans (Writer)
In 2000, Robin wrote *A State Affair* for Out of Joint. It went on two national tours, had two runs at Soho Theatre and was invited to be performed in the House of Lords. His most recent play, *The Arab Israeli Cookbook*, was performed at the Gate Theatre (2004). He co-wrote *Cobham Harbour* at the Half Moon Theatre; *Bet Noir* (Young Vic); *Sinners and Saints* (Croydon Warehouse); *Will and Testament* (Oval); and *Not Today Thank You* for Capital Radio. As an actor, Robin has appeared in eighty plays, thirty-six of them in London, with work at the National Theatre, the Royal Court, the Royal Shakespeare Company, Hampstead, the Tricycle, the Bush and the Young Vic. He has made thirty television appearances and been in twelve films.

Max Stafford-Clark (Director)
Founded Joint Stock Theatre Group in 1974 following his Artistic Directorship of the Traverse Theatre, Edinburgh. From 1979 to 1993 he was Artistic Director of the Royal Court. In 1993 he founded Out of Joint. His work as a director has overwhelmingly been with new writing and he has commissioned and directed first productions by many of the country's leading writers.

Johanna Town (Lighting Designer)
Other tours for Out of Joint include: *Macbeth* (also Arcola/Wilton's Music Hall); *Duck* (also Royal Court); *The Permanent Way*, *She Stoops to Conquer*, *A Laughing Matter*, *Our Lady of Sligo* (also RNT); *Shopping & Fucking* (also Royal Court/West End); *Feelgood* (also Hampstead/West End); *The Steward of Christendom* (also Royal Court & Broadway). Johanna has been Head of Lighting at the Royal Court since 1990 where her many lighting designs include *My Name is Rachel Corrie*, *The Woman Before*, *Food Chain*, *Under the Whaleback*, *Terrorism*, *Plasticine*, *Fucking Games*, *Just Stopped By To See The Man*, *Mr Kolpert*, *The Kitchen*, *Ashes and Sand* and *Where Do We Live*. Other freelance lighting designs include *Guantanamo*

Bay (New York/West End/Tricycle); *Someone Who'll Watch Over Me* (Northampton Theatre Royal); *How Love is Spelt* (Bush Theatre); *I.D.* (Almeida & BBC 3); *Six Degrees of Separation, Ghosts, Misfits, Richard II* (Royal Exchange); *Badnuff, Mr Nobody* (Soho Theatre); *The Dumb Waiter* (Oxford Playhouse); *A Doll's House* (Southwark Playhouse); *Brassed Off* (Liverpool Playhouse/Birmingham Rep); *Popcorn, Les Liaisons Dangereuses* and *Playboy of the Western World* (Liverpool Playhouse); *Little Malcolm & His Struggle Against the Eunuchs* (Hampstead/West End); *Rose* (RNT/ Broadway); *Via Dolorosa, Top Girls* (West End) and *Arabian Nights, Our Lady of Sligo* (New York).

Elyse Dodgson (Royal Court Associate Director – International)

Elyse Dodgson has been on the artistic team of the Royal Court since 1985. She was initially Director of the Young People's Theatre and has been an Associate Director and Head of the International Department since 1993. She has initiated play development projects in many parts of the world including Brazil, Cuba, France, Germany, India, Mexico, Palestine, Russia, Spain and Uganda. Much of this work has been produced at the Royal Court.

Scilla Elworthy (Peace Direct)

Terrorists and Peacebuilders

Max Stafford-Clark was a student at Trinity College Dublin at the same time as a rather odd girl called Scilla Elworthy. She was immersed in social studies and setting up hunger strikes on O'Connell Bridge while he was whirling around in the wild world of Dublin theatre. But they did enjoy some good parties together, and well... they went separate ways.

We know what became of him, but she has been less in the news. Scilla worked In Africa for ten years, joined the UN and then, perplexed by the spread of nuclear weapons, set up an organisation to find out exactly who made decisions about them.

Twenty-three years and three Nobel Peace Prize nominations later, this organisation can quietly bring together nuclear warhead designers with those who would roast them – Greenpeace, CND and the like. Its daughter organisation, Peace Direct, supports mediation between governments and insurgents, between perpetrators of violence and their victims.

One day Max saw her name in connection with David Edgar's play *The Prisoner's Dilemma* and got in touch. They started talking, and *Talking to Terrorists* is what they talked about.

Contact: www.oxfordresearchgroup.org / tel: 01865 242819;

or: www.peacedirect.org / tel: 0845 456 9714

Terror: WHY? by Scilla Elworthy and Gabrielle Rifkind will be on sale from Out of Joint (0207 609 0207 ojo@outofjoint.co.uk) and at the Royal Court Bookshop.

OUT OF JOINT

out of joint

In 2004, Out of Joint celebrated 10 years since the company's inaugural productions, *The Queen and I* by Sue Townsend and *Road* by Jim Cartwright.

Out of Joint is a national and international touring theatre company dedicated to the production of new writing. Under the direction of Max Stafford-Clark the company has premiered plays from leading writers including David Hare (the author of *The Permanent Way*), Caryl Churchill, Mark Ravenhill, Sebastian Barry and Timberlake Wertenbaker, as well as first-time writers such as Simon Bennett and Stella Feehily, whose *Duck* for Out of Joint was 2003's hit in Edinburgh, London and Dublin.

Blue Heart, Out of Joint/Royal Court 1997, Photo by John Haynes

'You expect something special from the touring company Out of Joint... here's to their next ten years' *The Times 2004*

Shopping and Fucking, Out of Joint/Royal Court 1996, photo by John Haynes

Touring all over the UK, Out of Joint frequently performs at and co-produces with key venues including the Royal Court, the National Theatre, Hampstead Theatre, the Liverpool Everyman & Playhouse, Soho Theatre and the Young Vic. By co-producing its work the company is able to maintain an on-going repertoire as well as premiering two new plays a year. Out of Joint is classed as one of the British Council's 'flagship' touring companies, and has performed in six continents – most recently in Sydney, Australia with *The Permanent Way* in early 2005. Back home, Out of Joint also pursues an extensive education programme, with workshops in schools, universities and colleges.

'Max Stafford-Clark's excellent Out of Joint company' *The Independent 2004*

Out of Joint's challenging and high profile work has gained the company an international reputation and awards including the prestigious Prudential Award for Theatre. With a continuing commitment from Arts Council England, Out of Joint continues to commission, develop and produce new writing of the highest calibre. Out of Joint's most recent production was *Macbeth*, set in a war-torn African state. The production transformed old mills, factories, backstage areas, a stately home and an 1850s music hall. It will tour overseas in 2005.

Macbeth, Out of Joint 2004, photo by John Haynes

'Out of Joint - a must-see company' *Time Out*

OUT OF JOINT

THE COMPANY

Director	Max Stafford-Clark
Producer	Graham Cowley
Marketing Manager	Jonathan Bradfield
Administrator & Education Manager	Natasha Ockrent
Assistant Director & PA to Artistic Director	Naomi Jones
Literary Associate	Alex Roberts
Finance Officer	Sandra Palumbo

OjO EDUCATION WORK

Out of Joint offers a diverse programme of workshops and discussions for groups coming to see our performances. For full details of our education programme, resource packs or *Our Country's Good* workshops, contact Max or Tasha at Out of Joint.

FREE MAILING LIST

For information on our shows, tour details and offers, call us on 0207 609 0207, email ojo@ outofjoint.co.uk or send your contact details to Out of Joint, 7 Thane Works, Thane Villas, London N7 7NU, letting us know whether you'd like to receive information by post or email.

Out of Joint is grateful to the following for their support over the years:

Arts Council England, The Foundation for Sport and the Arts, The Baring Foundation, The Paul Hamlyn Foundation, The Olivier Foundation, The Peggy Ramsay Foundation, The John S Cohen Foundation, The David Cohen Charitable Trust, The National Lottery through the Arts Council of England, The Prudential Awards, Stephen Evans, Karl Sydow, Harold Stokes and Friends of Theatre, John Lewis Partnership, Royal Victoria Hall Foundation

PAST PRODUCTIONS AND TOURS:

2004 *Macbeth* by William Shakespeare
Sisters, Such Devoted Sisters by Russell Barr

2003 *The Permanent Way* by David Hare
Duck by Stella Feehily

2002 *A Laughing Matter* by April De Angelis
& *She Stoops to Conquer* by Oliver Goldsmith
Hinterland by Sebastian Barry

2001 *Sliding with Suzanne* by Judy Upton
Feelgood by Alistair Beaton

2000 *Rita, Sue and Bob Too* by Andrea Dunbar
& *A State Affair* by Robin Soans

1999 *Some Explicit Polaroids* by Mark Ravenhill
Drummers by Simon Bennett

1998 *Our Country's Good* by Timberlake Wertenbaker
Our Lady of Sligo by Sebastian Barry

1997 *Blue Heart* by Caryl Churchill
The Positive Hour by April De Angelis

1996 *Shopping and Fucking* by Mark Ravenhill

1995 *The Steward of Christendom* by Sebastian Barry
Three Sisters by Anton Chekhov
& *The Break of Day* by Timberlake Wertenbaker

1994 *The Man of Mode* by George Etherege
& *The Libertine* by Stephen Jeffreys
The Queen and I by Sue Townsend &
Road by Jim Cartwright

CONTACT OUT OF JOINT

7 Thane Works, Thane Villas,
London N7 7NU

Tel: 020 7609 0207
Fax: 020 7609 0203

ojo@outofjoint.co.uk
www.outofjoint.co.uk

THE ENGLISH STAGE COMPANY AT THE ROYAL COURT

The English Stage Company at the Royal Court opened in 1956 as a subsidised theatre producing new British plays, international plays and some classical revivals.

The first artistic director George Devine aimed to create a writers' theatre, 'a place where the dramatist is acknowledged as the fundamental creative force in the theatre and where the play is more important than the actors, the director, the designer'. The urgent need was to find a contemporary style in which the play, the acting, direction and design are all combined. He believed that 'the battle will be a long one to continue to create the right conditions for writers to work in'.

Devine aimed to discover hard-hitting, uncompromising writers whose plays are stimulating, provocative and exciting. The Royal Court production of John Osborne's Look Back in Anger in May 1956 is now seen as the decisive starting point of modern British drama and the policy created a new generation of British playwrights. The first wave included John Osborne, Arnold Wesker, John Arden, Ann Jellicoe, N F Simpson and Edward Bond. Early seasons included new international plays by Bertolt Brecht, Eugène Ionesco, Samuel Beckett, Jean-Paul Sartre and Marguerite Duras.

The theatre started with the 400-seat proscenium arch Theatre Downstairs, and in 1969 opened a second theatre, the 60-seat studio Theatre Upstairs. Some productions transfer to the West End, such as Terry Johnson's Hitchcock Blonde, Caryl Churchill's Far Away and Conor McPherson's The Weir. Recent touring productions include Sarah Kane's 4.48 Psychosis (US tour) and Ché Walker's Flesh Wound (Galway Arts Festival). The Royal Court also co-produces plays which have transferred to the West End or toured internationally, such as Conor McPherson's Shining City (with Gate Theatre, Dublin), Sebastian Barry's The Steward of Christendom and Mark Ravenhill's Shopping and Fucking (with Out of Joint), Martin McDonagh's The Beauty Queen Of Leenane (with Druid), Ayub Khan Din's East is East (with Tamasha).

Since 1994 the Royal Court's artistic policy has again been vigorously directed to finding and producing a new generation of playwrights. The writers include Joe Penhall, Rebecca Prichard, Michael Wynne, Nick Grosso, Judy Upton, Meredith Oakes, Sarah Kane, Anthony Neilson, Judith Johnson, James Stock, Jez Butterworth, Marina Carr, Phyllis Nagy, Simon Block, Martin McDonagh, Mark Ravenhill, Ayub Khan Din, Tamantha Hammerschlag, Jess Walters, Ché Walker, Conor McPherson, Simon Stephens, Richard Bean, Roy Williams, Gary Mitchell, Mick Mahoney, Rebecca Gilman, Christopher Shinn, Kia Corthron, David Gieselmann, Marius von Mayenburg, David Eldridge,

ROYAL COURT

photo: Andy Chopping

Leo Butler, Zinnie Harris, Grae Cleugh, Roland Schimmelpfennig, Chloe Moss, DeObia Oparei, Enda Walsh, Vassily Sigarev, the Presnyakov Brothers, Marcos Barbosa, Lucy Prebble, John Donnelly, Clare Pollard, Robin French, Elyzabeth Gregory Wilder and Rob Evans. This expanded programme of new plays has been made possible through the support of A.S.K. Theater Projects and the Skirball Foundation, The Jerwood Charity, the American Friends of the Royal Court Theatre and (in 1994/5 and 1999) in association with the National Theatre Studio.

In recent years there have been record-breaking productions at the box office, with capacity houses for Joe Penhall's Dumb Show, Conor McPherson's Shining City, Roy Williams' Fallout and Terry Johnson's Hitchcock Blonde.

The refurbished theatre in Sloane Square opened in February 2000, with a policy still inspired by the first artistic director George Devine. The Royal Court is an international theatre for new plays and new playwrights, and the work shapes contemporary drama in Britain and overseas.

PROGRAMME SUPPORTERS

ROYAL COURT

The Royal Court (English Stage Company Ltd) receives its principal funding from Arts Council England, London. It is also supported financially by a wide range of private companies, charitable and public bodies, and earns the remainder of its income from the box office and its own trading activities.

The Genesis Foundation supports International Playwrights and Young Writers' Festival.

The Jerwood Charity supports new plays by new playwrights through the Jerwood New Playwrights series. The Skirball Foundation funds a Playwrights' Programme at the theatre. The Artistic Director's Chair is supported by a lead grant from The Peter Jay Sharp Foundation, contributing to the activities of the Artistic Director's office. Bloomberg Mondays, the Royal Court's reduced price ticket scheme, is supported by Bloomberg. Over the past eight years the BBC has supported the Gerald Chapman Fund for directors.

TALKING TO
TERRORISTS

First published in 2005 by Oberon Books Ltd
521 Caledonian Road, London N7 9RH
Tel: +44 (0) 20 7607 3637 / Fax: +44 (0) 20 7607 3629
e-mail: info@oberonbooks.com
www.oberonbooks.com

A catalogue record for this book is available from the British Library.

PB ISBN: 978-1-84002-562-0
E ISBN: 978-1-84943-582-6

Printed, bound and converted
by CPI Group (UK) Ltd, Croydon, CR0 4YY.

Visit www.oberonbooks.com to read more about all our books and to buy them. You will also find features, author interviews and news of any author events, and you can sign up for e-newsletters so that you're always first to hear about our new releases.

Contents

Characters

AN EX-MEMBER OF THE IRISH REPUBLICAN
ARMY (I.R.A.)

AN EX-MEMBER OF THE ULSTER VOLUNTEER
FORCE (U.V.F)

AN EX-MEMBER OF THE KURDISH WORKERS
PARTY. (P.K.K.)

AN EX-MEMBER OF THE NATIONAL RESISTANCE
ARMY, UGANDA. (N.R.A.)

THE EX-HEAD OF THE AL AQSA MARTYRS
BRIGADE, BETHLEHEM. (A.A.B.)

EDWARD, a psychologist.

PHOEBE, a relief worker.

AN ARCHBISHOP'S ENVOY.

AN EX-AMBASSADOR. (AMB.)

A BRITISH ARMY COLONEL.

RIMA, a journalist.

NODIRA, a dancer.

EX-SECRETARY OF STATE. (S.S.1)

ANOTHER EX-SECRETARY OF STATE. (S.S.2)

HIS WIFE.

CAROLINE, a landowner.

JAD, FAISER, MOMSIE, AFTAB, Luton Muslims.

A BETHLEHEM SCHOOLGIRL.

LINDA, MATTHEW, MICHAEL, a Foreign Office Committee.

JOHN, a husband.

MARJORY, a cleaner.

DERMOT, a bodyguard.

WAITRESS IN DUBLIN.

INGRID, a carer.

A number of names have been withheld or changed at the request of the interviewees.

Act One

MARJORY enters with a vacuum cleaner, cleaning up shards of plastic which litter the carpet. The S.S.1 comes in, slightly unsteady on her feet. She indicates that the hoovering should stop. MARJORY turns off the hoover.

S.S.1: I'm sorry, Marjory, do you think you could do upstairs? Sorry about this...I thought we'd get this done before you got here. It's our Labrador puppy...he eats everything in the house. I'm sorry Marjory, is that alright?

MARJORY: That's alright, I can do upstairs and finish this later.

S.S.1: It's not putting you out?

MARJORY: No, no, I'll do upstairs and come down later.

MARJORY goes.

S.S.1: I'll leave the dog next door. We've had to take the phone out of here; he ate the phone. And he's a terrible farter.

I got on with terrorists on both sides 'cause I treated them as human beings. They were mostly normal working-class men...I had an affinity with them. People said it was my gender...it wasn't...it was my class... that's what did it...I used to say to them, 'Don't call me Secretary of State, call me by my Christian name.' I shook their hands...none of my predecessors shook their hands. I didn't have a voice like: 'wonderful to see you.'

Talking to terrorists is the only way to beat them. I can't understand why Tony didn't understand that. Gerry and Martin wanted to talk; of course they'd done dreadful things, but they've got wives, they want to play with

23

their kids, they're normal family men. I wanted to appear as normal as possible. Mind you, it was fucking difficult…I had the Special Branch, I had security, I had the R.U.C., all men…wherever I walked I had this phalanx of men, like a tail, following me. I ran away twice. When I was staying at Hillsborough Castle which I shared with the Queen, darling, there was a pub half-way down the hill…

(*Calling off.*) John!

JOHN: (*Off.*) Yes?

S.S.1: You wouldn't make us some coffee would you? There's some bourbons somewhere. There's one Hobnob left but that's mine.

Distant sound of hoovering.

Ask Marjory if she wants a cup.

It was hard for both sides…they were bigoted, prejudiced, distrustful, fearful. I had to treat them as kids in a way. If I did something for Sinn Fein, like the Bloody Sunday Enquiry, I had to do something for the other side…an extra seat in the European Delegation, or access to Blair immediately.

JOHN comes on.

JOHN: I can only find one Hobnob, it's in three bits.

S.S.1: Makes no difference to me.

JOHN goes.

S.S.1: I was just left to get on with it. Cabinet meetings? You must be joking. I wish I could have taken my knitting in. Cabinet is a completely vacuous structure, and that's partly why I left. You'd walk in, sit down… Tony would say what policies he'd got in mind… ten minutes…totally vacuous, 'Speak'; then Gordon

would speak with more 'Speak'…six to eight minutes;
Jack Straw occasionally…he thought he was important
enough…that was 'Speak'. If Clare or Robin spoke that
would have content, but Tony and Gordon just nodded.
There was no other forum; Ali and Mandy made most
of the decisions; if I really had something urgent to say I
would tap Tony on the shoulder on the way out. I talked
to Bertie Ahern as much as I talked to Tony.

*JOHN comes in with a crumpled paper: the remnants of a
biscuit packet.*

JOHN: Is this what you meant?

S.S.1: Thanks.

JOHN goes.

S.S.1: I've been saving this. When Paisley walked out, I
thought, 'Thank God.' He wouldn't let anyone else
speak, he just shouted them down. The other thing
I thanked God for was the Women's Coalition; they
helped me with the seating arrangements. You couldn't
have a Shinner next to a Loyalist, you couldn't have a
Shinner next to the U.U.P., but with my two old fogies
from the Labour Party, and the Women's Coalition,
I had enough people to put between the people who
wouldn't sit next to each other.

JOHN comes back in with the coffee.

I don't miss it. I miss the car. The car meant John and
I could go out in the evening, and we could both get
pissed. Some ex-ministers have two cars; I got none;
and no security…they took it away the day I left
government. We've got nothing out here.

JOHN gives the cup of coffee to his wife. Her hand is shaking.

S.S.1: Thanks darling. Fuck, I've slopped it. We said, 'Can
you do anything for us out here?'

JOHN: They put in panic alarms.

S.S.1: We took them out last week. They kept going off.

We're miles from anywhere out here.

JOHN goes.

S.S.1: I've never been afraid. When I was at Hillsborough I used to walk in the grounds. If a sniper wanted to he could have got me any time. We used to have wild parties. I didn't invite Gerry and Martin 'cause that meant I'd have to invite the other lot as well. The most important thing…I was an ear listening. You have to allow that they believe in what they're doing.

PHOEBE comes on together with EDWARD, a psychologist, who breezes on. There is a comfortable chair into which he eventually settles. He takes off his coat and scarf.

EDWARD: I think I gave my peak performance last time… this may be something of a matinée performance.

S.S.1: Tony seems to have learned nothing from history. If you want them to change their minds, you have to talk to them. They won't do it very willingly because they don't trust you, but yes, you have to talk to terrorists.

Exit.

PHOEBE: It's really difficult for me to talk to you because…well…because what do you say when you return from interviewing children who were abducted by men who raped them, or nailed their knees together to stop them running away… Do you talk about the weather? And how do you talk about it without sounding sanctimonious or preachy? In the past, I…I…I suppose I've given up really…just slotted back into conversations about how hard it is to get a good cleaner.

EDWARD: Ninety per cent of the population aren't
enormously involved in politics; what are they doing?
They're taking the kids to school, they're watching
EastEnders...on the whole they're not watching plays...
they drink a bit, read a bit, have a bit of sex. When
they see a politician on the television, their first thought
would be, 'Would I get into bed with him?' When
they saw Thatcher they thought she was a bit bossy,
Howard's a bit creepy, they used to like Tony but now
he's a bit iffy... That's the ninety per cent.

PHOEBE: Save the Children is a child rights organisation.
Increasingly children are being used as combatants
by armed groups. They're cannon fodder. What we're
trying to do is negotiate their release. But to give you
some idea...there are twelve thousand child soldiers
in Liberia alone, and all the child agencies combined
have a capacity for dealing with two thousand. It's a
strange world I inhabit, meeting the extremes of human
behaviour. It's certainly easier to be there, feeling you're
doing something...

EDWARD: Ten per cent of the population do things...

PHOEBE: But even that's complicated, because in many
emergencies you are just one of the headless chickens.

EDWARD: Ten per cent. They're the movers and shakers.

PHOEBE: There have been times when I felt I was able to
do something, and that brings an extraordinary sense of
achievement and energy.

Exit.

EDWARD: It does look as if terror groups have a dynamic.
They always start with a radical thinker...a dreamer,
a proper intellectual with a sense of history; and a
grievance. 'Look at the year 1500. The Arab world
were leaders in philosophy, astronomy, medicine,

mathematics…and look how badly we're doing now.' It puts me in mind of Al Qutb. He formulated his radical new version of Islam on the campus of an American University. He sees all these scantily-clad cheerleaders…becomes sexually aroused. So he concludes, 'The fundamentals of our religion have been sidetracked by Western decadence.' People who want to cancel out a culture have to convince themselves it's worth destroying. The 9/11 terrorists went to topless bars when they were learning to fly in Texas. It's like me going to a country and instead of, you know, going to the Museum of Modern Art, I go into all sorts of sordid dives. I allow myself to enjoy the experience before feeling righteously indignant. But then this is a very hard culture to be sexually pure in. The teenage years are hard enough, but for young Muslims in Luton it must be intolerable.

A bookshop inside a mosque in Luton. FAISER, MOMSIE, JAD (older) and AFTAB are sitting on the floor. They are in stockinged feet.

FAISER: I don't do any of that foolishness I used to do a few years back…like chirping gals in the weekend… doing tings with dem.

MOMSIE: What you gotta remember bruv is that I went to hell, took a holiday there, and still came back; and I'm not going there again.

FAISER: Getting mash up on booze and drugs…

MOMSIE: Ravin', gal, booze and drugs / …madness, pure madness.

AFTAB: When I was young, I was in a state of confusion, and was not even aware of the foolishness / I was playing at.

MOMSIE: Bro, I went into prison a nutter and came out a Muslim.

FAISER: It hits you, bang, like bang bruv...what am I doing with my life?

AFTAB: We was all brought up here; you learn to walk like / ...

MOMSIE: / walk like, talk like...

AFTAB: Talk like, and like all the other kids you rebel / ...

FAISER: Rebel / more...

MOMSIE: / rebel more

AFTAB: 'Cause the background is...

MOMSIE: / Strict.

AFTAB: Strict.

FAISER: You know like Monday to Thursday, sort of normal...then four day benders...

AFTAB: Everyone's doing it so it must be good.

FAISER: It's like Robbie Williams bruv...he's had it all, all the cars, the women, and he's saying like, 'I've had enough. I don't know what to do, but I've had enough of that.'

MOMSIE: He should come here. (*Laughter.*) No seriously / he should come here.

AFTAB: You're right bruv, he should.

FAISER: Can you tell me that you could concentrate or keep your mind calm if you open a magazine and see an image of a naked lady / or some sexual reference?

MOMSIE: Can you believe this...I was with my father... it was ten o'clock yesterday morning, we was watching

T.V. and a naked man runs across the screen? / Can you believe it?

FAISER: This girl asked me the other day what I thought about gays. I said Allah was very clear about this. Gays must be taken to a high point and thrown off / ...

MOMSIE: When they're dead bruv...

FAISER: Oh yes, this is when they're dead. If they are not crushed, they must be taken to a higher point and thrown off. She was quite shocked by this, but I told her, 'There is no choice with Islam...you either believe it or you don't.'

AFTAB: You can't pick and choose.

FAISER: 'Oh I like this bit, but not that bit.'

MOMSIE: But it's better that you're gay and Muslim than just gay. When you're thrown off your high place as a Muslim, you'll be forgiven and rise to Allah's kingdom.

FAISER: If you're gay and an unbeliever, you'll rot and burn for all time.

JAD: The images of naked men and women are rife... visible to innocent eyes. There is already enough temptation within man due to his weakness of mind, body and spirit, even when he is in good surroundings. Islam is a way to keep pure and on the path.

FAISER: Exactly bruv. I'm not saying that acting or cinema is evil, or the people that frequent those places; but what I am saying is that I cannot be present in these places. The reason being dis. In the theatre people are gonna be smoking...

AFTAB: Drinking alcohol...

FAISER: And maybe talking about lewd subject matter. I do not want to be privy to this type of behaviour. It's an internal battle to control the desires of your spirit, which are more times leanin' to do selfish and foolish tings...

JAD: Rather than helpful to your loved ones, your community, or, of course, yourself.

MOMSIE: If me and an attractive lady end up in a room together, something might happen...you know bruv...

FAISER: You might feel something...

MOMSIE: But if me, you and you were in a room, I might feel it but I can't do anything. / So it's about prevention.

AFTAB: It's about prevention.

JAD: This mosque is about peace; and the removal of temptation.

FAISER: All sorts of people come in here...kids doing their homework...people who just want to sit and think.

MOMSIE: Some people have been asked to leave.

Frissant.

FAISER: Some of our people are no longer welcome. We made that very plain. Last year during Ramadan, this one guy Rafeeq started shouting his mouth off, saying our leaders were preachin' a weak message, / weak and westernised.

JAD: You correct yourself first, then your family, then other people.

FAISER: He says it's okay to be robbing from non-believers...any non-Muslim house...their wealth is permissible 'cause you're in a land of war...it's a holy war... 'cause Blair is attacking Muslims in other parts of the world...

AFTAB: He's saying you can't attack Muslims abroad and pretend you like them at home.

FAISER: He says you can go all-out, man…killing innocent women and children…any tower block… Canary Wharf…it's a legitimate target.

MOMSIE: We sat down and told him to go, for spreading rubbish amongst the youngsters.

FAISER: It's because of Rafeeq I'm afraid to send my wife to the centre of town. He generates so much hatred it's unbelievable. I was on the pavement last week…this old guy winds down his window and shouts, 'Oi, F Bin-Laden!'

AFTAB: Is that F or F with an 'ing' on the end.

FAISER: With an 'ing' of course. I said, 'Stop your car and come round and speak to me.' But he didn't. He said, 'F you mate' and drove off.

JAD: Of the Muslim community in Luton they're not even one per cent…the fanatics…but they're listened to more than the rest of us put together. That we're a community and work well together, where's the news in that?

Exit.

FAISER: Sex, lies and videotapes…

MOMSIE: Sensationalism is the buzzword bruv.

FAISER: 'I'm a celebrity, get me out of here'. You're only gonna match that by having a guy with a hook in his arm preachin' rubbish.

His mobile phone rings.

Sorry, I gotta take this. The bumper's in the alleyway… The headlights are in my bedroom / actually they're in my brother's bedroom… My mum's going ballistic…

Three hundred... It's a good offer, think about it.

MOMSIE: How many Muslims are there worldwide? Two
and a half billion. That's a million million, then half of
that again. How come they find the two guys what are
chattin' rubbish? What would you think if I found the
one white guy who preached death to all Muslims in the
world and I said that's what all white people thought?

They go. EDWARD comes back on.

EDWARD: So, I want to start a group – 'Psychologists
against four-wheel drives in Chelsea' – a small group
committed to violence, with the objective of blowing up
all the four-by-fours in SW3. There are a lot of people
who have an uneasy feeling that something is not
quite right. I come along and put my finger on it, 'Well
you see, I enjoy walking to work, but now there are
Jeeps and Subarus crushing 2CVs...disabling dilatory
pedestrians; and they represent the worst aspects of
blatant consumerism.'

The revolutionary thinker never gets very far...but I've
sown a seed in one of you...a pragmatist. The dreamer,
the thinker, that's me, retires to the background as a
guru. You organise the politics of the movement, select
an inner group, and delegate responsibilities. 'You,
you and you, go out and slash some tyres.' A terror
group is usually small...very small...you probably
only need thirty activists, supported by two hundred
semi-activists...people to provide safe-houses and run
messages...and loosely supported by two thousand who
disapprove of violence but who are generally in favour.

If, when you leave the theatre, there's a stall on the
pavement, 'Stop Animal Vivisection' and there's a
monkey on the table with its eyes pinned open, quite a
lot of you will give money without supporting someone
who fire-bombs a laboratory in Cambridge. The

difference between a terrorist and the rest of us really isn't that great.

So a member of my Chelsea Gang will fire-bomb a Range Rover...sales will temporarily dip...but then firebomb a Volvo C 90 with a dog in the back...and every paper will run the picture. Someone'll be hauled up before the Security Services, and the first question will be, 'Are you a member of PALC?' (Psychologists Against Land Cruisers.) It's interesting...it's always the interrogators who provide terrorists with their vocabulary. The movement will continue if it can recruit enough people to the cause. I can guarantee that if one of you goes out now and knocks on a hundred doors, ninety-nine people will tell you to get lost, but you'll just happen upon someone in crisis; someone who's bright but blocked. Within a week you will have imbued that person with the joys of tyre-slashing. It'll be something like joining a cult...cut their hair, give them an orange robe, you'll convince them they are now extraordinary. Ordinary people don't have a dream in their heads... not like them...not like the people you're going to meet.

Lights up on I.R.A., U.V.F., N.R.A., P.K.K. and A.A.B.

EDWARD: I'm just going to nip out and get a double espresso.

N.R.A.: My father had a farm. The goats I liked.

P.K.K.: We had a mountain farm. In the winter the snow came up to the roof. You used the warmth of the animals to heat the house.

N.R.A.: My goats were so young they thought I was their mother. Their names were Kitanga and Kozi.

P.K.K.: When the snow was deep we dug a tunnel to the well in the middle of the village. Very poor, but happy in spirit.

A.A.B.: We made a football out of rags...

U.V.F.: Using jumpers as goalposts.

A.A.B.: And we used to play this game... 'Soldiers and Thieves'... The thieves threw pebbles at the soldiers; if they caught them, they beat them up. Sometimes we called it 'Palestinians and Israelis'. Only the unpopular boys got to play Israelis.

I.R.A.: My father moved from Belfast to Norwich to work in a heavy-engineering plant.

U.V.F.: We moved to a place called Suffolk Park. We would go hurdling over the hedges and have our own wee Grand National.

I.R.A.: My childhood seemed happy to me. The whole family went to the Hippodrome in Great Yarmouth. All I remember is a lot of corseted women high-kickin' in frilly skirts.

U.V.F.: Twelve to fourteen, sex and cigarettes. You'd a went to a disco...getting' your first kiss...

At that time you'd a been talking about Slade and company. I used to have long, long hair...as people did in those days...so I was a bit of a Noddy Holder myself.

A.A.B.: One day...my mother was sweeping the little yard at the front of the house. Six Israeli soldiers came round the corner and one of them kicked me from behind. I landed like a pancake. My mother said to the soldiers, 'Why are you doing that to my son?' The soldier said, 'What's a whore like you doing outside your house in a curfew?'

N.R.A.: My father was the only parent I had. My mother had left. I wanted him to touch me; the only touch I could get was when I would wash his feet. I was always looking down. I only remember the basin... It was blue.

P.K.K.: The government say no more money for Kurdish villages in the mountains. We move to a town…nine of us living in one small room. We didn't speak Turkish; our clothing was different. At school, no-one, no even teacher, spoke to me. I am left in corner alone.

Re-enter EDWARD with coffee.

N.R.A.: One time…I was eight years old…my stepmother said, 'I'm going out, you had better cook the dinner.' I thought how the beef stew looked when she made it. I put nearly half a kilo of cream into the sauce and some curry; it had the right colour…it looked as it should. My stepmother told me to take it to the dining-table. My father, he sat there and shouted, 'Woman, is this the food you have prepared?' My stepmother said, 'Ask your daughter, she cooked the food. No-one asked her to, but there it is.' My father, he told my brother, 'Go and get me chillies.' My father put all, every one, into the food, stirred it round and told me, 'You eat it now.' I thought, 'He's going to beat me anyway,' so I just sat there. He shouted at me, ordering me to eat. I still sat there, looking down. He told my brother to fetch a stick…the big stick for beating cows…he told me to lie down. I put my hands on my bum to protect me; he busted my fingers. He never cared if I died or not. I wished to die so the police would arrest him. He beat me on the head…I've still got something, look. Then he jammed my head between his legs, gripped tight, couldn't breathe, beating me, beating me…my stepmother moving the chairs so he could beat me more easily…my brothers and sisters screaming, 'Stop, stop… father, you're killing her…stop, stop…'

Silence. She passes her thumb across her forehead several times.

Eyes close. Tears.

When my father finished, I was full of blood.

A.A.B.: By the age of thirteen, our game 'Soldiers and Thieves' had become a reality. We threw stones at a jeep that was running past our school. I was caught. I was sent to prison for six months.

N.R.A.: It was the last day of school. Sofia, my best friend, came running. 'Don't go home…I heard your father's going to beat you again.' She took me to her house. I showed her mother my busted fingers. I said, 'If you send me home I will drink Belmeth…it's what they put in the dip when they treat the animals.' I stayed with her that night. The next morning she showed me a photograph of my real mother and told me the journey to find her. I got on a bus. I left home. I was eight.

I.R.A.: My grandfather was dying of cancer. I was thirteen. I came back to Belfast to see him. Paisley had just led his first venture, marching up the Falls Road and demanding the removal of the tricolor. Three days of serious rioting. It made a big impression on me.

U.V.F.: Lenadoon Avenue… I helped people pack up their furniture…old people, people who had no interest at all in violent conflict. Over five hundred residents were put out of their houses at that particular time.

I.R.A.: I went to my aunt's house in Andytown. Every night they'd been down behind the settee, what with bullets flying around.

U.V.F.: On one occasion I was out walking m'dog. It was a little mongrel dog, it was a lovely little dog…but the reality was I came under attack by a crowd. They near hit my dog with a bottle, and I charged at them. It was one of those situations where you took a mad rush of blood to the head. A guy stepped out from the crowd and fired shots. I had to jump over a hedge. The little dog didn't know what was going on. He run beside me, and I grabbed ahold of the dog.

I.R.A.: They were hairy days.

A.A.B. When I left prison the first time, I formed a stone-throwing group. But we were children…we were naïve…we had our meetings in the street.

It was after midnight…I was with five of my brothers, sleeping on mattresses on the floor. Every two mattresses shared one dark grey United Nations blanket, made you scratch all over. I opened my eyes… there was an M16 pointing at my head. Every one of us was screaming. My mum was crying. The soldiers were silent, calm. The officer said, 'Your son is the ringleader.' I was taken to the army compound.

He said, 'Your mum is a bitch do you know that? She must be a bitch because your dad fucked her and produced a dog which is you.'

I said, 'Your mum must have been fucked by loads of guys to produce a pig like you.'

He said, 'You think you're a man, don't you?'

I didn't say anything.

'Well, let's see how much of a man you really are.'

He drew back his leg and kicked me as hard as he could in the balls. I started screaming. I couldn't breathe.

He said, 'You see…donkeys…you all end up screaming like donkeys.'

I was put in prison for six years. I was fourteen.

N.R.A.: It was the middle of the night. I had been walking a long time. I saw a flash of light, then a man's voice… 'Stop! Who are you?'

'I'm looking for my mother.'

'Where's your father?'

'He's dead.'

'You'd better sleep here.'

He threw two blankets on the ground.

She does.

A group of men came out of the bush…they had guns on their shoulders. The blankets were smelling bad, but there were swarms of mosquitoes. I lay down and covered my head.

She lies down and goes to sleep, folded in the blankets.

EDWARD: I know I've got to stop drinking coffees but I keep putting it off. It's the thought of all that nettle tea.

Now…I'm going to say two words and you can only answer 'safe' or 'dangerous'. I don't want you to think about it. Right…lettuce.

ALL: Safe.

EDWARD: Good. And now…shark.

ALL: Dangerous.

EDWARD: Yes, but you see the interesting thing is that adolescents wait a bit before they say 'dangerous'. This is the key time to recruit. Adolescents are such good material…they can see how things could be different, but aren't aware of practicalities…so they're slightly reckless and have a strong illusion of immortality.

P.K.K.: I was fifteen when someone came to talk to my elder brother. I met them as well.

I.R.A.: Both my grandparents were in the I.R.A.…joining the movement was the most natural thing in the world. I felt myself truly at home for the first time in my life.

U.V.F.: It was a question of me defending my area against

people that were demonstrating aggression towards my family, my friends and my neighbours.

P.K.K.: We called ourselves the Kurdestan Revolutionaries. We met at weekends. There was no drinking, absolutely none.

I.R.A.: Sixteen and seventeen year-olds were given positions of responsibility. There were plenty of photographs of Che Guevara.

EDWARD: People are more aware of status in their teenage years... 'Where am I in the pecking order?' Being in a committed organisation...well, you're all winners now. 'Oh hello Edward, what are you doing with yourself these days?' 'Oh, you know, I'm still at the Middlesex.' 'Oh,' they say, 'still at the Middlesex,' and walk on. But unbeknownst to them I'm torching a jeep every month. This has given my self-respect a tremendous boost.

It's also a time of enormous peer pressure, particularly with sex. If you're not very good at pulling girls, the recruiters give you a way out...who needs girls when you've got status?

P.K.K.: A member of the older group would take five or seven of us and instruct us in the history of Socialism. The first books we studied were Karl Marx...Dialectical Materialism and Historical Materialism. If we had been caught we would have been sent to jail or tortured.

U.V.F.: The first meeting I was at, there were four of us... we discussed the safety of the area basically. By now we were coming under daily attack...violence was visited upon me.

I.R.A.: The meetings took place in an upstairs room at the back, or the kitchen. People would arrive singly.

P.K.K.: For two years I am attending meetings, and also start distribute leaflets. In crowded places you could give them into people's hands. Our town had at least one secret agent in every street...this is much danger.

EDWARD: You can give adolescents the feeling they're shaping history; 'You think you can change the world... well, yes actually, you can...I'll show you how.'

I.R.A.: Gun lectures...an Armalite...how to strip it...how to maintain it.

P.K.K.: The older group said to counter violence from the State, there's no alternative but to use violence.

U.V.F.: I had a gun put in my hand at the grand old age of sixteen. I near shot the man who put it there. The only thing I'd ever fired was my finger coming out of the cinema...here I was at sixteen with this bloody big weirdy weapon.

I.R.A.: Bomb lectures.

U.V.F.: Petrol bombs.

EDWARD: Most of us have a lot of things furnishing our minds...I'm giving evidence at a public enquiry in the morning, but then I mustn't forget we're having a dinner party on Thursday, going down to Wiltshire at the weekend, got to get the boiler serviced. Terrorists certainly aren't thinking about the day after tomorrow. They're enjoying the moment. Even if it's ghastly, it's invigorating. It's what's called a 'peak experience'.

I.R.A.: A lot of anger. The turnover was very high...people killed, interned...

P.K.K.: The P.K.K. was formed...the Kurdish Workers Party...

I.R.A.: We were losing friends.

P.K.K.: There was a Member of the Turkish Parliament; he was also landowner…he was protected by his twenty personal guards, and a private army of two hundred. He just took whatever he want…people's crops, their animal…he would drive a hundred k., go into a house, take the daughter, keep her for two months, and then give her to one of his guards and say, 'Fuck her.' He once threw five P.K.K. activists into a…nasil soylenir? Patoz bugda ile samani ayirir.

A.A.B.: (*As interpreter.*) An ladim 'patoz'. Threshing machine.

P.K.K.: Threshing machine. And you know the worst? This man was original a Kurd. We decide to target this man. To hit him is to hit the State. Ten o'clock at night, thirty of us creep up. The guards outside are silenced with gun to head and gagged. There were several doors into the main living-room…we arrive all at once…there is the fascist eating with his guards, not family…we shout, 'This is a raid…don't move.' The guards open fire. My friend next to me is shot dead. As soon as M.P. realises situation, he hid behind two of his men; they were both killed; by now there were so many bullets, we ran into the night.

I.R.A.: 10th June 1973…a Sunday. I was in Sparmount Street. There was a house I was going to lie low in for a few hours. I was a hunted man at this stage. I got to the front door…the door was locked. The people had gone on the coach to a commemorative march for Wolfe Tone.

EDWARD: Psychologists are always fascinated by people who achieve a timeless state of concentration, a total absorption. What we have with the hunted man is an enforced total absorption.

I.R.A.: I knew where there was a spare key…but there was a look-out post on top of a tower block overlooking

Sparmount Street…six paras came round the corner… there was no messing about…up against the wall…I.D. search…I had false I.D….they knew who I was…

P.K.K.: One of our guys got caught. I had to go up into the hills with two friends. It was winter. We lived in caves. And then one morning…hardly light, bitterly cold…I was first to hear it…the noise of an engine. Then we saw them…the blue berets of the soldiers. They are lined up in the shape of a crescent moon.

U.V.F.: It was called the Conway Bar. Our intelligence had told us that an I.R.A. unit was meeting there. We took two stolen cars…four of us, two guns, one bomb. It was a mixture as was often the case in those days, possibly fertilizer and bleach; it was in a metal gas container, two feet in height, and it had a standard fuse…fifteen seconds from lighting to detonation. We arrived about eight p.m., basically at the front of the building… nobody in sight. We got out of our cars, two of us carrying guns, one carrying the bomb; the fourth guy stayed in the getaway car with the engine running. The plan – light the bomb, throw it through the door, go.

We were huddled in the door, three of us, trying to light the bomb. At that particular point the door opened, and my colleague swung round and fired a number of shots into the bar. I basically raised my weapon to take aim, as our third colleague was pushing the bomb between our legs. The movement or whatever it was caused the bomb to explode prematurely.

Basically I came round with half the building on top of me, with my clothes blown off, barely able to see or hear. I didn't know what had happened to anybody; there was a heavy pall of smoke. I picked myself up and made my way towards what I thought was the getaway car, but it drove off. Apparently the getaway car had already got away…the driver thought we were dead. I

43

made my way up the street, staggering absolutely; and at that particular point another crowd, a republican crowd…there would have been I.R.A.among them I'm sure… came out from another bar very close by. I got into a railway tunnel, and thought I was concealed in the darkness. I heard the words, 'There's the bastard there'…and I lifted my head and turned round and at that point I was seeing the flames on my back. The crowd was coming after me…I got to the edge of Belfast Lough and they caught me. Well they didn't shake my hand and welcome me, as you can imagine. They proceeded to beat the living daylights out of me, and they were bringing me back across a bridge to hang me…they were going to hang me from that bridge… when the military police arrived. I've never been so happy to see a policeman in my life.

P.K.K.: For the first hundred days of interrogation we were completely naked. The women were raped, most of the men had batons shoved up their arses, or forced to sit on beer bottles 'til they disappeared up.

U.V.F.: The Military Police threw me over the bonnet of their car and smashed my face in; and then handed me over to the R.U.C., and the R.U.C. beat me about the place on the bonnet of their car.

P.K.K.: When they put electrodes on your testicles you faint. When they attached them to your hands and feet, it feels like the flesh being ripped off the bone. At the end of the interrogation, the guards tell us we have been sentenced to death. I am told to put aside the clothes I want to be hung in. I choose a red T-shirt. Red's my favourite colour.

U.V.F.: The R.U.C. took me to Greencastle Police Station. I was lying in a heap, badly burned, bruised and bloodied…a police medical officer ordered them to take me to the hospital immediately.

P.K.K.: The President take off my sentence from death to twenty-one years. There are sixty-seven files awaiting the Parliament. Even Turkey cannot hang sixty-seven without creating international fuss.

I.R.A.: There was just me in a corridor with three Military Policemen…two of them were sitting, the third was walking up and down. At one point as he was passing, I got this almighty crunch in the base of my spine. I went straight down. A British military medic examined me. He looked at my back. He said, 'What happened there?' 'Nothing.' He said, 'You've been duffed up lad.' Those were his very words. And he touched it…no pressure… just touched it, and my knees went from under me. He slipped me a couple of paracetamol. Then I was interned in Longkesh.

U.V.F.: Fifteen years I was in Longkesh Prison Camp. One colleague died six weeks later as a result of his injuries, and the guy driving the getaway car was killed in an internal Loyalist feud. Seventeen people were injured and one woman was killed. When I heard a woman had been killed, it near tore a hole in my heart.

P.K.K.: Twenty-one years and four months I was in prison. Now when I say it, it shocks me. All my youth…all my early life…gone…just gone.

Exit.

I.R.A.: Going to prison was the start of my further education.

Goes to the back to change into envoy.

U.V.F.: I read everything and anything.

A.A.B.: Psychology, politics, I read about Nasser and The Suez Crisis, Marx, Engels, Irish history, the political history of Colombia, American history.

U.V.F.: There was a lot of exploration in relation to Irish history that went on. Our leaders encouraged us to understand our enemy.

A.A.B.: I must have read one thousand five hundred books in seven years.

Exit.

U.V.F.: We converted metal beds into shotguns. We were making alcohol that would have sent rockets to the moon.

EDWARD and U.V.F. leave. The ENVOY comes on very quietly so as not to disturb the sleeping N.R.A. He has on a heavy coat and a scarf.

ENVOY: I got up at something like four in the morning… 'cause it was very heavy snow. I got up before the family woke and I thought, 'Well, I'll be back in seven or eight days,' and I never said goodbye to them. Only just got to Heathrow 'cause the snow was so heavy…got the plane into the Lebanon, and that was it. That was it for five years.

Lights up on RIMA.

RIMA: I'm Lebanese originally, and…er…I think journalism came knocking on my door because we had civil war in Lebanon, and, by the way, by training I am a chartered accountant, and I was actually auditing Price Waterhouse…no I was with Price Waterhouse auditing Associated Press, and Terry Anderson who was bureau chief then, before he was kidnapped, said, 'Don't you find this boring – why not join us…work for us?' They needed someone who could speak both Arabic and English to monitor the radios in the evenings.

ENVOY: I took bodyguards from the airport into town and a short-wave radio so that I could pick up signals from Terry Anderson's flat, where I was staying. That evening the phone rang. 'We're the people you want to see, come and meet us,' and they named a place. Well you can't just go out and meet…it's dangerous out there. I said, 'First of all…'…yes, crikey, I'd forgotten this… this is stranger than fiction…I said, 'Before we go any further, will you give me the nickname of a girlfriend of a friend of Terry Anderson's.' I knew full well that to get that obscure bit of information they would have to be in contact with Terry Anderson or at least with one of his guards. After two hours they phoned back. 'The name's Christo.' That was the right name, and the next night I agreed to go and see them.

RIMA: So I started doing both, but I didn't have a clue about journalism…I mean I knew vaguely about political issues…like my first time I called Terry Anderson I said, 'There's big news.' And he goes, 'What?' And I said, 'They've postponed the baccalaureate exams.' He said, 'Rima, if there's a car bomb, fifty killed, call me…otherwise don't bother.'

ENVOY: I went to a doctor's waiting-room. He said, 'You've asked to see the hostages; we're going to let you see them 'cause they're sick and very depressed.'

I said, 'Look, if I come with you, you'll keep me.'

He said, 'We will not keep you.' He gave me his hand on this. He stretched out his hand.

I said I needed twenty-four hours to think about it. He agreed.

Really the decision had to be mine. If the hostages really were, you know, sick…how sick? What if I didn't go and one of them died?

I went back the next night. As soon as I walked in, the telephone rang. The doctor said, 'I'm sorry, there's an emergency at the hospital.' In fact he left at that moment.

I thought, 'Well, if I've come this far, I might as well go through with it, you know.'

A few minutes later my contact stepped into the room. I was given a quick body-search, we went down in the lift, got into a car, changed cars, then I was blindfolded, and we went into a safe-house. Over the next three days we moved from house to house, they said to shake off a tail; and finally, on the fourth day, I was put into a van, blindfolded, and driven across town. We came to what I believed was an underground garage. In the floor was a trapdoor. He said, 'Jump down.' The door closed behind me, and, when I took off my blindfold, I was in a tiled cell. I was no longer a negotiator...I was a hostage.

RIMA: Beirut at this time was described as a place with The Plague. Kidnapping was huge. All the bureau chiefs had to move out. We ended up having to run the entire situation.

ENVOY: For the first year they interrogated me about Iran Contra. It was one of those occasions when, you know, you were just glad you didn't know anything. They weren't too brutal. They used to beat me on the soles of my feet with cables.

RIMA: Then I got married in Beirut...fantastic wedding. My husband's an Englishman who was with the *Mail on Sunday*. Sixteen armed guards. It is so dangerous I make him dye his hair black.

ENVOY: One evening they told me I had five hours to live...and actually I was so exhausted...I really had been interrogated a lot...I was feeling...in those sort of circumstances, the body just takes over, and I slept... and after five hours they came back. They said, 'Do you want anything?' I said, 'Yes, I'd like to write some letters to my family and friends.' They said, 'You can write one letter. Do you want anything else?' 'Yeah, I want a drink.' My throat was dry, I suppose because I was afraid. I also had this strange out-of-body experience…I was responding to their questions in a very faltering, haltering, hoarse sort of way; and yet looking at myself from the outside, I thought, 'You're answering boldly.' They said, 'Do you want anything else?' I said, 'Yes, I'd like to say a prayer.' I said The Lord's Prayer, that's all. It could have been an occasion for great histrionics, you know, 'I pray for the forgiveness of these people,' but I think that's all in The Lord's Prayer, you know. They said, 'Are you ready?' I said, 'Okay.' They said, 'Face the wall.' I was turned round…a gun was put to my head…then they dropped it and said, 'Another time.'

RIMA: We used to get people from the *Evening Standard* …they would call us and say, 'We want to talk to the terrorists, do you have a number for Islamic Jihad?' And you would say, 'One moment, let me look it up in the…' and you would sit there thinking, 'Do they have any idea, these people?'

ENVOY: I think then the decision was made to release me. What they did was they dressed me as an Islamic woman. We got to this house; I was meant to be a relative coming from the country; so the family came out to greet me, and they even brought a little child out, and of course this child took one look at this bearded giant in women's clothes and screamed.

No, I'm sure I was going to go home at that stage… then something happened in the outside world. I can't prove this, but it's the time Salman Rushdie published *The Satanic Verses.* I went back into normal hostage accommodation for another four years.

RIMA: So my future husband, he's an Englishman, and his friend…I'm not belittling them…I mean they were part of the *Mail on Sunday*…came asking me, 'Where's Terry

Waite?' And I said, 'Just go down the road, turn left, second on the right, across the road, you know there's a building there, and he's in there.'

Exit.

ENVOY: What you learn in strict solitary is…Okay, I'll make an inner journey. It's dangerous of course, because you can easily get swallowed by the darkness we all find within ourselves. I didn't indulge in *ex tempore* prayer, for fear I might just get to the point of saying, 'God, get me out of here.' So my prayer would be very simple. 'Lighten our darkness we beseech thee O Lord, and by thy great mercy, defend us from all perils and dangers of this night.' I was in captivity for one thousand seven hundred and sixty-three days altogether. From their point of view it was quite a creditable achievement.

I'd have been quite happy if I'd been left with a great pile of books of my own choice. I actually asked the guards to bring me books…and …um…they wouldn't. They said, 'We've only read the Koran, we've never read any books at all.' Eventually I came across a guard who was more sympathetic, but he couldn't read English; and he couldn't be seen going into an English bookshop. So he used to work through a series of cut-outs…people who had no knowledge of the other parts of the chain. One day he came in the cell…he said, 'I've got a book for you.' I said, 'Oh thank goodness.' He went out, I lifted the blindfold, and I laughed out loud… he'd brought me *Great Escapes* by Eric Williams. The second book was even worse; believe it or not it was *A Manual of Breast-feeding*…it wasn't even illustrated; and then when he brought me Dr Spock, *Baby and Childcare*, I thought, 'My God, somone has got fixed on the Baby and Children shelf; how do I get him on to something more interesting?' I peered beneath the blindfold and

I drew a picture of a penguin, and said, 'If you see that on the front of any book, buy it.' About two weeks later he brought me *As I walked out one Midsummer Morning* by Laurie Lee.

The ENVOY goes. Bright morning light. Sounds of birdsong (African).

N.R.A.: When I woke there were kids doing drill...the youngest was six. It was so exciting...arms left, right, left, right, left, right, left, right, left, right, left, right, left...Muku sawa... Attention! Muri legeza... Stand at ease! Muku sawa... Attention! I wanted to join in.

Enter COLONEL and EX-AMBASSADOR.

AMB.: My second posting was to Accra as Deputy High Commissioner...that was great fun because I played a very central role in the Sierra Leone peace negotiations.

COLONEL: I've also recently been highly involved in Sierra Leone, as an expert witness in the U.N. sponsored, war crimes trials. I'm a colonel in the army...in charge of doctrine. My job is to evaluate the wars the British Army is engaged in so that I can draw lessons... because...er...one of the great difficulties is that, inevitably, we tend to prepare for the last war. Nobody now is going to compete with the Americans in conventional warfare, because...er...plainly...er... you're always going to lose. I mean, their marine corps alone is the size of our whole army. Therefore the chances are the British will find themselves in more and more peculiar engagements, and people need to be sufficiently flexible to respond. Let's make this quite clear. I don't fight...my soldiers fight...my job is to make sure they win.

AMB.: I was locked in a hotel in Togo for five weeks with a most extraordinary bunch of people...Foday Sanko and five or six others famous for chopping off babies' limbs;

you'd got President Eyadema of Togo hosting it…as far as I know he's the only head of state who murdered his predecessor with his own hands…an interesting claim to fame…he strangled him in bed. I was sitting with these people one day, and I thought, you know, 'For certain, I think, I'm the only person in this room that hasn't killed anyone.'

I was bloody terrified most of the time. They were all fuelled up on heroin, which made negotiating difficult.

N.R.A: The third day I was allowed to join in…two hours marching, then how to dismantle an AK 47, and what to do in case it jams. The AK 47 was bigger than most of us kids, so we charged with wooden sticks. The Resistance Army was short in men, so the training didn't take long.

AMB.: During the negotiations, I formed a friendship with one of the guys, who'd done terrible things…but he'd been kidnapped at the age of eight and taken into Liberia to fight with Charles Taylor. He was nineteen by this time…three years earlier he would have been regarded as a child soldier…someone to be pitied, but, having passed the age of sixteen, he became a war criminal. He seemed sure that after this, Sierra Leone would return to normal and he would go to college; he's almost certainly been hung.

COLONEL: Living in the jungle, the guerrilla armies had no vehicles, no transportation; so they had the most enormous requirement for labour. And so whenever they moved through a village, they simply abducted everyone. They just took them.

The young boys and girls were sent to training camps. They often had to kill their parents to show they were loyal.

The guerrilla armies developed their own initiation, which passed on the ability to become bullet-proof. You had to pay sixty leones, about twenty pence to a special witch-doctor. The initiation was quite, was quite, er… arduous. They were given various fetishes and told to observe a whole series of taboos.

At the end of three days they'd come back to the initiation grounds, where they'd be lined up…a hundred, two hundred, whatever…and the witch-doctor would empty out an AK47 magazine at the line. Those who died showed they had failed to keep the taboos. The AK47 tends to kick up when fired so I suspect most of the bullets went up in the air. The witch-doctor was a crap shot. I mean it would only be three out of a hundred or so that would die…but the others would be bullet-proof as long as they kept the taboos. If you touched a woman for example you lost your bullet-proofness; you weren't allowed to eat snake; and the fetishes…they were each given leather pouches containing…typically it would be the unborn foetus of a…a…a… I mean, pregnant women seem to have a particularly tough time of it.

N.R.A.: A month later I was picked for a special assignment, along with a few other kids. The commander told us to go sit in the middle of a dirt road and pretend to be having a good time playing with the sand. A convoy guarded by government troops came along…we just carried on playing. The first truck stopped right in front of us. Most of the soldiers jumped down. We ran back to our fighting group who opened fire. I'd never heard a noise so loud…it was the rocket-propelled grenades hitting the trucks. I would have run away if some of the other kids hadn't held me down. After it was over, everyone ran to the dead soldiers…I had no idea people could loot from the dead…but ripping underwear off corpses soon became part of everyday life.

Those who had surrendered had their arms tied behind their backs so that their ribs stuck out. They were shot dead.

COLONEL: Amputations were conducted as a matter of course. It was called 'sending a letter'. You'd find someone returning from the fields, cut off one of their arms, and say, 'This is a letter to the village…we're coming back tomorrow, we will want food.' It was absolutely just standard. Acceptable. And that has got to cause you to think about, you know, the nature of terror and who are the true perpetrators, because in this environment amputation had become commonplace.

N.R.A.: We would say, 'Short sleeve, long sleeve?' and we would cut at elbow or wrist.

COLONEL: So I guess that the true criminals are not the people who exact the crimes, but the person who first thought it was a good idea.

N.R.A.: One day, Salem Saleh, Museveni's younger brother, told us, 'Prepare yourselves…tonight you are to attack a government camp…it's four kilometres away.' I meant to get some sleep, but would it come? No. I let it go.

Using the light of the moon and stars, we walked through the bush until we found our soldiers already in position. We waited. I was being bitten to death by mosquitoes, but all I could do was chew my lips. Then it happened…the first rapid fire of an AK 47…that was the signal…to kill each and every thing in the camp. 'No living thing' was the order.

COLONEL: This is a society where human sacrifice is still quite common. So when you've got this kind of culture, it's not surprising that they are given the order 'no living thing'.

N.R.A.: Men and women began running out and dropping in one big mess, still naked, their clothes swinging from their hands. The massive fire of our guns drowned out everything...the screaming of the goats and hens and people...eventually silence...nothing. Then daylight.

We entered the camp...there was just one big bloody heap of goats and hens, soldiers and their women who had been on a visit...all dead in the morning sun.

Back in our camp the prisoners were made to dig their own graves. One of our officers told me, 'Go spit them in the eye.' He told them, 'No bullets will be wasted on you. After you have dug your grave, I will call my best men. They will hit you on the head with an akakumbi.' That was a short, heavy hoe. They stood two at a time, and our strongest men smashed their foreheads and the backs of their heads until they dropped in the grave and died.

Enter PHOEBE.

PHOEBE: It's hard to understand the impact on most children because they switch onto survival mode.

N.R.A.: We killed with total commitment. We fought; we tortured...we thought that was the best way to please our bosses.

I was supervising torture at the age of thirteen.

PHOEBE: It was astonishing...no crying...no laughter... they were just very quiet and concentrated...they were surviving.

N.R.A.: Looking back now, I don't know how I did survive. We used to joke, 'Am I coming back tomorrow?' We grilled a whole chicken before attacking a convoy. Might as well...going to be dead in half an hour.

I used to look into the eyes of the Afandes, the senior officers; did they give a damn about us? One day

Museveni came to talk to us, he told us we were fighting for freedom, as if there were any freedom to fight for.

COLONEL: When a guerrilla army moves, there's an advanced guard, then the main body, and then there'll be a group of families, at least the same strength as the army itself. But then eventually the…er…the…er…the penny dropped; these weren't families at all…they were slaves. And most of the…er…the women were there for the soldiers to have sex with.

N.R.A.: They called us names like 'Masala ya wakubwa' or 'Guduria'…it meant female soldiers were the fodder of Afandes, the big stew-pot all the officers could eat from.

I had sex with Kashilingi…he would say, 'Nine o'clock, my room.' I would stand to attention and say, 'Yes Afande, sir.' No words were said during sex. It was like sleeping with death. I would come in, put my gun down, take off my military uniform, have sex, put my uniform back on, pick up my gun and walk out. I wanted to like him as a father, not a sexual thing. Later, when I saw him in prison, this huge man cramped in a tiny cell, I felt sorry for him, but still scared…sorry, scared, sorry, scared, sorry, scared…

Many of my child comrades started to lose their mind. Some of them ended up turning the gun on themselves. If you could find the road, you could leave, but you would be a deserter.

PHOEBE: The majority of deserters were brought back and executed by their own friends.

N.R.A.: We couldn't give them mercy. We had to think the same way…all of us. We increased our brutality to gain more ranks.

AMB.: I'm spending Christmas…I'm in the process of splitting up with my wife…I met someone on my next posting in Tashkent…there was a spate of ridiculous stories in the press about impropriety because my new partner…well, she's…she's…um…she's younger… considerably younger than my wife. Anyway there's an awful lot to sort out…saucepans, bed linen. My wife and I…there's nothing acrimonious; we're going to use the time over Christmas to sort out the logistics, that's all.

Exit.

COLONEL: My epiphany moment came much later than it should have done, perhaps. I was twenty-eight. I was in Northern Ireland. Actually it was Christmas time. I realised that if I had been born in Crossmaglen or South Armagh, I would have been a terrorist. And that's an understanding every soldier should have. None of this is personal.

The COLONEL goes. They pass EDWARD coming on. EDWARD collects his coat and scarf.

EDWARD: The key to the ideology of violence is to see your enemy as sub-human.

They're only Jews, gays, blacks, not normal in any sense of the word.

N.R.A.: 'Think of them as animals…look at them…they speak a different language, they're dark, black, and very evil. Think of them as scary things…you'll find it much easier to kill them.'

Exit.

EDWARD: We've got a cottage down in Wiltshire. We're going there for Christmas. Can't wait.

Exit.

PHOEBE: In Rwanda, two years after the events, people started going barmy. It's only when you're back in control of your own life that you have the luxury of falling apart. A good sign is when the kids drop the names they've given each other – 'Rambo' or 'Captain Blood'. They've obviously been desperate for attention under all the atrocity and when we give them some they start to laugh and cry again. Two years ago I adopted my own little boy. He has his own sad story…but he's doing so well now. On Tuesday we're going to a carol service in Guildford.

PHOEBE goes. The scene segues into a coffee-bar in a Dublin shopping-mall. Canned Christmas carols, twinkly lights, decorations.

A.A.B. is at a table with his minder, DERMOT. DERMOT is studying the racing page.

A.A.B.: 1993 was a good time. People are working, supporting their families. We started to think of peace. And the question you have to ask is, 'Who killed Rabin? Was it a Palestinian?' No, it was an Israeli.

I start working for a peace organisation as a policeman for the Palestinian Authority. And on first day of Intifada, when I am in Jericho, there was a big demonstration.

A.A.B.: Civilians started to throw stones at the Israeli soldiers. The Israelis started shooting gas, then plastic bullets, then real bullets. I was sitting on a doorstep with a friend. A six year-old boy came and sat by me. He look at me. 'You have a gun, why aren't you using it?' The last he told me, 'If you are too shy to use it, I will shoot them.'

Me and my friend started shooting at the soldiers. There was T.V.…they put my picture there, and after that I was on their 'most wanted' list.

A WAITRESS comes to the table with a cup of tea and a slice of cake.

WAITRESS: Is that the Leopardstown race you're lookin' at? The big hurdle.

DERMOT: Yeah.

WAITRESS: Emerald City, that's the one...Paul Carberry's riding it.

Exit.

DERMOT: Emerald City is it? Right.

DERMOT goes back to reading, and eats the cake.

A.A.B.: We started defence of our homes, my family, my house...and we joined up with friends from other cities, which Israelis would call Terrorism. My friends chose me to be leader of Al Aqsa Brigade in Bethlehem because I have lot courses in security, I know more info about guns, the army we face. Three times they try to assassinate me. The first time is in Jericho. How do they know where I am? You tell me. They have spies everywhere; they tell the army what time we come, what time we leave. Yes, I have killed a spy; I will not in detail talk about death. But we will talk about the life.

After this I escape to Ramallah. I stay there six months. Someone is tapping my mobile phone. The next thing I am offered a car...a very good car at a very cheap price. Of course it is cheap...it has a bomb inside.

DERMOT: (*Overhearing.*) That's a good one.

A.A.B.: Me and my two bodyguards are in a car in Bethlehem. Rassan was driving. It was a '97 Chevrolet, grey...two in the afternoon...nice day, no cloud, no nothing; we were on the road called the Bethlehem – Hebron. My friend called me on the short-wave radio and said, 'Be careful, there are helicopters.' And maybe two minute, through the windscreen, just a dot in the sky. I shouted to Rassan, 'Stop the car, stop the car, very

quick!' He scrunch the brakes…we run from car very
quick…we'd got about ten meters…two missiles hit the
car…I feel myself fly another ten meters.

DERMOT: Jeez…I've not heard that before. What about
the car?

A.A.B.: What do you think? A fireball.

DERMOT: You'll be alright for a minute, will you?

A.A.B.: You go to horse shop again?

DERMOT: Yeah, yer auld one says Emerald City…she's
usually right.

He goes.

A.A.B.: He's my minder…Dublin Special Branch.

Israel attacked Bethlehem with two hundred tanks, ten
thousand soldiers, and four Apache helicopters. They
shoot me in the leg. I will show.

He starts to remove his shoe and sock and roll his trouser leg up.

A friend of mine start to drag me…very pain. We
cannot believe the tanks will come into the square; the
Church…the last refuge.

*Stands up and shows us his lower leg…it is hideously mangled
with a magenta scar three inches high and four inches wide.*

You see that's where the bullet went in…it exploded
inside the leg.

Putting sock and shoe back on.

Me and my friend were last into the church. Then
the door was bolted. My face was yellow. Everyone
thought I was going to die. I believe my God has given
me another life. Thirty-nine days we were inside the
Nativity Church. Thirty-nine days I lay in the exact spot

where Christ was born. A nun came every morning at six to clean the wound...I never in all my life forget that nun. The first day I get to shit was after twenty-five days. Don't ask me how I am feeling; it's like a woman having a baby. When I leave the Nativity Church I am thirty-eight kilos. I went in at seventy-six kilos. There were loudspeakers, day and night, 'Come out, we know you are wounded, we take you to hospital; give yourself up.' My health was getting worse. My friends said, 'Should we give up and go to the hospital?' I said, 'If you say this again, I'll cut my leg off.' They didn't say it again. In the end there was an agreement that the siege would end, if twenty-six of us were exiled to Gaza, and another thirteen to Europe. 10th May at nine in the morning, two buses pulled up outside.

At Ben Gurion airport we were handed over to British soldiers. This British Army doctor, this woman, a big woman, she just picked me up and carried me all the way to the plane, and started to operate on my leg straight away. We flew to Cyprus, to a civilian hospital. On 22nd May I left Cyprus for exile in Dublin.

My eldest son...he thinks Ireland is another town like Bethlehem. He asks, 'Why you not come home?'

My wife is called Zainet.

I have four children.

Uday...he is nearly six years.

Qusi...he is nearly five years.

Muhammad...he is three and a half years.

Samed...he is two and a half years. I have never seen him. He was born 22nd May, the very day I landed in Dublin.

What I feel for my sons is more than anything in the world.

A.A.B. is still. The carols play ('O little town of bethlehem'). A BETHLEHEM SCHOOLGIRL comes on with her homework.

GIRL: Christmas Day in Bethlehem. This is part of our homework...keeping a daily diary. But what am I to write? My dad said it would snow, but it only rained. We are under curfew, so I have to think how to spend my boring time. Well...I watched T.V. and listened to Backstreet Boys. I went to bed hoping that next Christmas would be a better day, 'cause I'm up to my head with these soldiers treating us like chickens.

The Christmas lights shimmer as the lights fade. They too fade to blackness.

Act Two

A penthouse flat with a view along the Thames to Canary Wharf.
Dusk. The EX-AMBASSADOR is seated at a table with his lap-top.
There is an unopened bottle of white wine on the table.

AMB.: When I was at university, reading history, it was
perfectly possible to believe in progress...you know,
The Tolpuddle Martyrs, the Chartists...a lot of dreadful
things in the last century, but then the Berlin Wall...

NODIRA comes in from the kitchen.

NODIRA: You want some pizza? Is home-made.

AMB.: It's not, is it?

NODIRA: No, I buy, but I add extra tomat', mushroom,
extra cheese, so will be very good like home-made.

NODIRA goes back out to the kitchen and comes back with
knives, forks and paper napkins. AMB. puts his laptop to
one side.

AMB.: But now it's a picture of regression. Do you know,
not since the early seventeenth century have we
sanctioned the use of evidence obtained under torture.
Even Mrs Thatcher...she was basically a libertarian. I'll
do that.

AMB. finds a corkscrew, takes the cork out, pours the wine.

AMB.: The only job being an ambassador trains you for
is being a wine-waiter; you know a lot about wine, and
you're sufficiently pompous.

NODIRA: When I'm a little bit drink, I shy not too much.
On Saturday I have an audition for Iranian Restaurant
in Hammersmith...is called Daddy's Restaurant. This
woman said, 'I want to see your talent.'

AMB.: Nodira loves dancing. She loves dancing all day long.

NODIRA: This is how we meet.

AMB.: We met professionally.

NODIRA: He saw my dancing.

AMB.: Something must have impressed me.

NODIRA: Yes, I was danced good.

AMB.: A dancing girl from Samarkand, believe it or not.

NODIRA: One time I'm trying to give interview, but they just said I was hairdresser, even though I can't how to cut hair. But truth I was English teacher for beginners and daytime, but, in the evenings I was belly dancer... belly not ballet... (*Laughs.*) ...Arabic.

She picks up a purple carrier-bag.

I have already costume, would you like to see? This very big... (*Large, silver-spangled bra.*) ...like for cow...

Laughs. Takes out a short silver skirt, totally hung round with small silver discs the size of five pence pieces.

If I follow noise of costume, my spirit quickly comes again.

She hands the skirt to AMB.

AMB.: (*Putting skirt to waist and gyrating hips.*) We have to find some innovative ways of paying the rent. I'm not going to be on a salary for much longer.

NODIRA starts to gyrate her hips. Her whole body sways.

NODIRA: When we meet in nightclub, every night he is not dancing, and I am always asking, 'Come and dance.' And then one night...oh...it is awful. He dance like...

(*Demonstrates and laughs.*) ...and I say, 'No, no more dance.'

AMB.: It's true actually, I'm not a very good dancer.

During the scene AMB. drinks most of the white wine. NODIRA gets out a needle and thread to adjust her bra, and sometimes goes to the kitchen to see to the food.

AMB.: I'd only been our ambassador in Tashkent one or two weeks when two things happened very quickly. The first was the trial of a gentleman called Khudaybergeinov...

NODIRA: Not 'k' – 'h'...Hudaybergeinov...it means 'God gift'.

AMB.: He was being accused of the murder of two policemen...um...the robbery of a jeweller and about five other things, including attempting to overthrow the government. Twelve other people had already been convicted of the murders...the policemen really had been killed...but when a murder happens, that's a jolly good reason to get rid of a couple of dozen political opponents by charging them all. It's what the Human Rights Watch call recycled crimes. There were five other defendants. Hudaybergeinov was charged with all the offences...the others with various combinations.

The trial was held in a very stuffy basement. The accused were inside a cage made of those iron poles you use in the making of reinforced concrete; it looked like someone who could weld a bit had knocked it up; and round it were...I counted them...seventeen guards with machine guns. It really made it hard to see the accused at all.

The judge kept making gratuitously anti-Muslim remarks. The uncle of one of the men had signed a statement saying the accused had discussed terrorist

activity and were being instructed by Osama bin-Laden.
And I recall the judge sort of interrupted and turned to
the accused… 'How could you conspire? How could
you understand what you were saying to each other
through your long Muslim beards?' It was just sort of
yelled. And all the policemen and cronies went, 'Haw,
haw, haw, haw, haw' as if it was the funniest thing
they'd ever heard.

There was a plea from the defence for the jeweller to
point out which three men robbed him, and as chance
would have it, he chose entirely the wrong three. The
judge interrupted and said, 'Sit down, sit down. Now
you other three stand up. Is it them?' And the jeweller
said, 'Yes.'

The uncle, who signed the statement saying they had
links to Al-Qaeda, was a typical country Uzbek…
varnished black skullcap, long white beard, long
traditional gown, maybe seventy years old. He was not
more than three feet away from me, and, as he gave
his evidence, he shook more and more, and at the end
he broke down and he said, 'It's not true…all I've told
you…it's not true. They tortured my children in front
of me until I agreed to give evidence.' And then he wet
himself; and without looking up, he said, 'We are poor
country people from Kokhand, what do we know of
Osama bin-Laden?'

Slight pause.

Hudaybergeinov was sentenced to death.

For me, the most affecting thing… as I was entering
Hudaybergeinov saw me…and there was this obvious
Westerner in a sort of three-piece suit, and you could
see…it's hard to describe…there was this momentary
gleam of hope…

AMB. drifts off into his own thoughts for a moment.
NODIRA runs her hand down the back of his hair, gets up
and takes the dirty plates out into the kitchen.

NODIRA: (*Going off.*) Would you like tea?

AMB.: Tea? Perfect, thank you. The second thing was the
arrival at the High Commission of some photographs.
One of the staff handed me an envelope and said, 'I
don't know if you want to look at these; if you do,
you'd better brace yourself, or have a strong drink.'
Inside were these close-up photographs of a corpse.
They were pretty horrible...the flesh had been severely
scalded, lurid red, and there was a close-up of the
hands which had had the fingernails pulled out. I
sent the photographs via the Foreign Office to the
Glasgow University Pathology Department. They sent
back a report which said basically this person had
been killed by immersion in boiling liquid while still
alive...um...the legs...um...and lower torso had been
immersed completely, and ...um...you could tell it was
immersion, not a sort of spattering or scattering, because
there was a clear tide-line.

The dead man had been a member of Hizbut Tehrir,
an Islamic sect a bit like the Moonies, and he had
refused to recant his religious beliefs, or to say, 'I made
a terrible mistake and here are the names of another
twenty people I wish to denounce.' So he was boiled
alive.

I discussed both these incidents with my American
counterpart...um...who was saying, 'Oh well, maybe
they go a bit far sometimes, but you know, the Islamic
menace is out there.' I felt I'd woken up in the middle of
Graham Greene's *The Quiet American.*

NODIRA comes back in with two cups and saucers. She
goes out, comes back with a jug of milk and a plate of iced

biscuits. Lastly she brings a teapot which she puts on a mat. AMB. munches a biscuit.

AMB.: I started sending things back to London saying, 'There is something unacceptable happening here and we can't continue going along with the American position.' This isn't a line which goes down very well in Whitehall lately.

Before I went out to Tashkent, I'd had a whole series of briefings about the 'War on Terror', but no briefing whatsoever on the human rights record of the Uzbekistan Government. I think you're supposed to ignore it, and that doesn't...you don't need any training for that.

The following November I received some intelligence material from MI6.

NODIRA: I didn't know him in this time.

AMB.: It was about the I.M.U., the Islamic Movement of Uzbekistan and their links to Osama bin-Laden... What this material said about armed terrorist units roaming the mountains above Samarkand just wasn't true. I thought, 'Some other poor bastard's been tortured.' So I asked my deputy to go to the American Embassy, because I could tell from the coding that this had been passed from the Uzbeks to the C.I.A., who had shared it with MI6...she went to see the head of the C.I.A. in Tashkent. He said to her, 'Yes, you're right, it almost certainly would have been obtained under torture...isn't that strange? That never occurred to me as a problem.'

I sent a telegram back to London saying, 'Look... practically, legally, and morally, I don't think we should be getting this stuff, let alone acting upon it.' I didn't get any reply...and then I got called back to a meeting in March 2003.

NODIRA: By now we have so many romantic moments.

AMB.: I knew there was going to be a showdown. I couldn't countenance…I wouldn't keep quiet about it.

On the morning of the interview I stopped at St James's Park tube station for breakfast. I had sausage, bacon, fried egg, fried tomato, toast and tea…the prisoner ate a hearty breakfast. The waitress was rather pretty…

NODIRA: Who?

AMB.: No-one. The waitress. She spilt tea over me.

NODIRA: You don't tell me this.

AMB.: It didn't matter.

NODIRA: There is so many you don't tell me.

Exit.

AMB.: While I was eating my breakfast, I found myself gazing idly at passers-by with a vague kind of love. It was my first day back in the U.K. I thought, 'These are my people. I love their resilience, their decency.' It was a Noel Coward moment. I had an overriding feeling that these people, quietly on their way to work, would be outraged if they knew what was really going on.

Enter LINDA, MATTHEW and MICHAEL. LINDA is described as 'very arid'; MICHAEL has spectacles on a string, 'fastidious and prissy'. MATTHEW, 'very expensive grooming, very push, didn't bother to open his mouth very wide'. They sit round the table. They have papers and folders.

AMB.: I got up…I hadn't been paying attention to the time. I left a tip, a generous one, two quid for the pretty girl who spilt tea down my trousers.

LINDA: You're late.

AMB.: Yes, I'm sorry.

LINDA: The Permanent Under Secretary apologises…an urgent meeting has come up. You know Matthew and Michael.

AMB.: (*To audience.*) Matthew was MI6, head of Whitehall Liaison…a link between the Intelligence Service and the Foreign Office. Michael…Sir Michael Wood, Foreign Office legal advisor, a thoroughly decent chap.

LINDA: The Permanent Under Secretary wishes me to assure you that your concerns have been given full consideration at the highest level. He has discussed this with Jack Straw and 'C'…

AMB.: (*To audience.*) 'C' is like 'M' in the James Bond films.

LINDA: 'C' has given his views. Both the F.C.O….

AMB.: (*To audience.*) Foreign and Commonwealth Office…

LINDA: …and MI6 have taken legal advice on the question you have raised. Michael, could you outline the legal position?

MICHAEL: I am not an expert on the U.N. Convention on Torture, but I cannot see we are in material breach of any provision simply by possessing, or indeed using, information obtained under torture, and subsequently passed to us. It does appear that under Article 11 such evidence would be inadmissible in a Court of Law, but that is the only restriction. Arguably we are further distanced by the fact that the material comes to us via the United States. I make no comment on the morality of the case.

AMB.: Michael, I have to say a number of prominent international lawyers have told me that the use of such material would be in breach of the Convention.

MICHAEL: There is certainly nothing on the face of the Convention to that…that…that effect, and I'm not sure

70

that I've seen anything published which…which…which would, which would confound my point of view.

AMB.: Michael, I think that / sort of legal nit-picking is…

LINDA: I think we have the legal view, and that is very plain. Michael, would you be so kind as to put it in writing and send it to the Ambassador.

MICHAEL: Certainly.

LINDA: Good. Now, Matthew, could you give the view of the Security Services.

MATTHEW: Certainly, Linda. This is high quality intelligence material; it plays a very important, a vital role in the 'War on Terror'. It would be a major loss if we ceased to have access to it. It would also cause unprecedented practical problems for the U.S. – U.K. Intelligence Sharing Agreement, which we are anxious should not be disturbed.

AMB.: But it's nonsense. The intelligence is crap.

Wincing, shifting of limbs.

It exaggerates the strength of the I.M.U. and is full of false information about so-called links to Osama bin-Laden.

MATTHEW: On the contrary, I can assure you this has been considered at the very highest level.

LINDA: Thank you. I think that clears that up. We needn't detain you, gentlemen. But if you would stay a moment, please.

MATTHEW and MICHAEL clear up their papers and leave.

LINDA: The Permanent Under-Secretary realises these are difficult times for many in the Service…this question of torture is very difficult; and he wants you to know that both Jack Straw and he lose sleep over it.

AMB.: It's alright for Jack Straw. I'm at the sharp end. I'm meeting people who…I don't think Jack Straw's sleep patterns are top of their concerns. You / should try being…

LINDA: We really do understand why you are upset. But we need to know that you are on message. I should not have to remind you that you act on behalf of the Secretary of State and in accordance with the policy of ministers.

AMB.: Yes, I understand the situation perfectly.

LINDA goes. NODIRA has drifted back into the room with the pizza.

AMB.: I got into such a state over all this I had a mental collapse and was hospitalised.

NODIRA: I'm not seeing you whole summer.

AMB.: I didn't get back to Tashkent until November. I arrived back on the Saturday of the rugby World Cup Final. I went straight to a bar where there's always an expat crowd…it's run by a very nice chap who's an Indian from Slough…got there just in time to see Jonny Wilkinson's drop goal…

NODIRA: You get back Saturday? But you not come see me 'til Monday.

AMB.: No…well, it was the final.

NODIRA: You not tell me you are back. Only now am I finding your secret.

AMB.: Darling, I came to see you as soon as I could.

NODIRA: Yes, for one hour.

AMB.: Nodira gets very passionate, I'm afraid.

NODIRA: Of course, I am artist.

AMB.: Yes indeed, darling.

NODIRA: But tell how I am also your partner.

AMB.: Yes, Nodira moved into the Embassy. She acted as hostess at some of the Ambassadorial parties and provided the entertainment.

NODIRA: I wear costume of nurse with mini-skirt.

AMB.: That raised a few eyebrows I can tell you. The whole business had absolutely flabbergasted me...you do wonder if this is how people slipped into ordering cattle-trucks to go to Auschwitz...

But then even weirder was the guy from the Security Services saying, 'This is valuable information,' and me thinking, 'No it's not. You know there aren't armed camps in the hills above Samarkand. It's not, it's not, it's not true.' But in their world it is true, because their world is full of Osama bin-Laden groups.

Enter COLONEL and RIMA.

AMB.: It's just the same as Iraq and the Weapons of Mass Destruction.

RIMA: Iraq is crazy; Iraq is scary.

COLONEL: It depends which Iraq you're talking about. It depends whether you mean the nice little war we fought and won so convincingly last year, or the rather more difficult situation we now face.

RIMA: I think every time I go to Iraq, every trip, there's something...there's a new element more frightening than the trip before.

COLONEL: We were bowled over by American over-confidence...the idea that Iraqis would welcome us with open arms and just needed a little help from us to become the model for a Middle-Eastern democracy...

all this kind of stuff, which is the Neo-Con spin
in Washington. As a result they were driving the
operational planning and we were just fitting in where
we could. It means that the post-conflict peace…we
don't use that term any longer because it implies that
there's an end to conflict…but, but, but the peace had
not been taken seriously. It's been likened to us, you
know, riding a horse with no reins, no stirrups, no
nothing…no control…and we're just taken to, to, to
wherever the horse wants to take us. And that's literally
the position we found ourselves in.

RIMA: There are two groups in Iraq now…insurgents, or
what you might call Freedom Fighters…and terrorists.
The insurgents say they solely kidnap people who
are working for the coalition; even a suicide attack
must have a specific aim, an objective. Whereas the
terrorists… 'We just want to die, it…doesn't matter…
We just want martyrdom.' These are the terrorists…they
place a car bomb; it kills four Americans and fifty Iraqis.
I think that's mindless.

COLONEL: The first time I went into the Bogside in
Derry I was terrified. I was commanding a platoon at
the age of eighteen. But you pretty soon lose that sense
of danger because the enemy will behave predictably…
it's possible to anticipate their moves. I knew the man
who tried to kill me. When I went back for my second
tour, I came across this man again and I immediately
thought, 'Thank God, I know you…you're the man who
tried to kill me.' But, of course, I wouldn't let him know
that. The…the…um…the hairy times always arrive with
new enemy commanders who have new methods.

RIMA: These new groups, you know, God, it will be a
one-way ticket; if they take you, that's it; at least with
the insurgents you think, 'Maybe I can pay a ransom, or
you can discuss…'

There were times we thought, 'God, if we're going
to be kidnapped, please not with this new lot. And
please, God, I'll beg of you, not with the knife, not the
beheading.' Having to watch the beheading, it was…I
can't tell you, it took forever…slicing, slicing, slicing…
even for a month I couldn't eat meat.

COLONEL: That's why I'm so horrified by the Israeli
army. When I've talked to them, I've tried to explain
how counter-productive it is to pursue a policy of…
um…of 'Destructuration', and by that I mean targeted
killing to destroy structures. All such murders do
is create a new enemy which you have to learn to
understand all over again.

You probably remember, last May we had six military
policemen killed in Iraq. London spoke to our
commander, 'Can you go in and do something about
it?' The answer was 'Yes, but there'll be an awful lot
of dead Iraqis in the morning.' Instead he decided to
go in and talk to the Sheiks and religious leaders, but
not to pursue the killers. I use that particular example
a lot when I'm lecturing to Americans because an
American officer would have been ordered to go in
from Washington whereas we let the commander on the
ground take the decisions…he's much more sensitive
to the situation. The guys from London or Washington
could easily order something that was inappropriate.

RIMA: What have the Americans done in Fallujah? All
you've done is have a beehive and you've dispersed all
the bees now. You knew where they were…now you
don't. So it's become more dangerous.

COLONEL: All you do is create yet more groups you
don't know and you don't understand. Is the power
and effectiveness of these groups being exaggerated
by politicians? I think the answer is…er…is…is…is
probably 'yes'. As for Iraq…catastrophic. But it's too

late now…it's a complete disaster. I'm not saying we will, but, oooh yeah, we face strategic failure.

Exit.

RIMA: We stayed with some insurgents. It was Ramadan, and there was about half an hour before the end of fasting. They said, 'You can stay as long as you cook for us.' So I said, 'Fine'…the market was still open…I said, 'Get some meat, get some vegetables,' and I walked into this kitchen and it was the most disgusting thing… the cooker was…I don't know…full of yuk; they had no salt, no herbs; and then these guys walked back with bagfuls of stuff and they opened…there's about eight or nine kilos of meat with fat like this, and then you can see some red.

There's one small knife that hardly cuts anything, and the gas things are not functioning properly, and Iraqi food…I mean forget Ramadan…on a daily basis they must have like a rice and a stew, otherwise they feel hollow. I put some oil, rice and tomato paste…I had to get it right because these guys, I was going to spend the night with them, and I had to make sure they were happy with me, so they protect me at least if anything happens, otherwise they say, 'She's a bad cook, take her.' So Ali, he's my fixer, and I did a stew of God knows yuk, and I did potatoes and salad, and one guy fixed up a gas ring to a big cylinder of gas, and I despatched two other guys, and they came back with black pepper and turmeric, and we put this in, and it became a sort of yellow stew of yuk, and the break-fasting call came…but you break fast with fresh dates… so I rushed out to have…my main thing is to have a cigarette…I sent a text message for my editor, 'Okay, I intend to spend the night in Fallujah. By the way I have to cook them dinner.' And he sends one back saying, 'Blimey, I can't believe what I'm hearing.'

The drones start about eight…they're small but very
loud like 'ZZZZZZZZZZ'…continuous, and at about
eleven the bombing started. In the first thirty-six
minutes there were thirty-eight bombs; and that night
we watched television, and Mr Bush won. Some of the
guys were saying, 'Who cares if Bush or the other guy
wins…the fact is anyway Iraq is lost. We've lost Iraq.'

After the thirty-eight bombs they said, 'Relax,
stop counting, there's more to come, make it as a
background noise'. They were very religious these guys.
They were sitting doing a lot of Koran; they believe
their lives were in the hand of God.

The Americans continued shelling 'til about five in the
morning, and then there were the minarets, the call to
prayer from a hundred minarets, and the drones at the
same time.

Suddenly, suddenly, ten past five…everything
stopped…not a shell, nothing…and then I slept for like
two hours. I was sleeping on the sofa which was also
very hard, smelling, and I think the mattress might have
these little things.

The plan was for me to stay on…we had bought
everything for the duration, but on that day something
personal happened that I wasn't prepared for…at all…
um…

If there were any chemists in Fallujah I didn't know,
and how was I going to tell those particular guys to
buy what I needed, I mean, what? It was not going to
sit right in lots of different ways; and the place I was
staying from cleansing point of view was just…it's the
hole in the ground…if that's clean it's fine…but if it's
dirty and yukky and smelly…and anyway we needed to
buy a generator and candles.

I decided we should go back to Baghdad... I was in my hotel and I heard they had sealed Fallujah completely, even the exit I had used to get out.

We heard that all the guys we stayed with had been killed by a bomb. I was crying maybe. They had been good to us.

Exit.

AMB.: I should say that as soon as I got back that November, I was extremely ill again...double pulmonary emboli...

NODIRA: I really didn't like that he's being Ambassador, because he lost his health in this system.

AMB.: ...from which I very, very nearly died...which is when I was rushed back to England...

NODIRA: But this you not tell me. I am hopeless.

AMB.: No, darling, I wasn't / able to...

NODIRA: I not drink, I not go out. I think now I must find another... and I have...I have been busy with another... he is Russian. But in one week, Stuart, his brother, call me. 'Don't worry, he is in hospital in England.' I thought it is kind of trick. I say to Stuart, 'Tell your brother everything is finished.' Then you write letter... 'I'm alive, I love you, you should be with me.' So again these romantic words.

AMB.: And I invited you to Germany for December.

NODIRA: And you open visa for me from Uzbekistan.

AMB.: Ah yes...got into trouble about that too.

NODIRA: I have never been in Europe, so I say, 'Okay, I will come.'

AMB.: May 2004, I'm doing the job much as I always did when the F.C.O. put out a circular following Abu

Ghraib to say that were anyone in the Service to have evidence of torture by U.K. forces or any of our allies, we should report it. So I sent a telegram saying we were 'selling our souls for dross', and raising all the points I'd been specifically warned not to.

I went on leave in August...I was due a lot of leave...I was just ready to go back at the beginning of October, when *The Financial Times* got hold of my telegram. Now, I hadn't leaked it and I strongly suspect the Foreign Office had; because I'm then phoned up that morning to say I've been withdrawn as our Ambassador to Tashkent because the leaking of the telegram would make it impossible for me to work with the Uzbek Government.

NODIRA: And I said, 'Good...it's okay. Now we stay in London.' Come on...is time for pills. Honest, if it not for me, he forget pills.

AMB.: It's true actually. I always forget.

AMB. and NODIRA go. Enter I.R.A. and CAROLINE.

I.R.A.: I'm sitting in a Nissen hut in Longkesh; I came to the conclusion that one bomb in London was worth more than a hundred bombs in Ireland. And, having lived in Norwich, I believed I could assume an English accent, which was vital. I couldn't do it now; certainly not with you listening, but if you can do it, you've got to do it. I was involved in several operations in England. I was there for months at a time. I'm not going to talk about the operational side of it at all...I've never talked about it...there are still ongoing issues. Let's just say from time to time you put a device in place and you would have no cause to go back.

CAROLINE: It sticks with you. I still wake up in the middle of the night...bolt upright...and it's always the same time....quarter-past, half-past three...

I.R.A.: I didn't sleep when I was on operations. You get worn down...the attrition, the constant fear of the knock on the door...usually the knock on the door comes between five and six, so you'd always be up at five in anticipation. I drank every night...four cans of beer... ended up fifteen cans of beer, just to get to sleep.

CAROLINE: I still think about it. What is it?...twenty years later...

I.R.A.: You have to assume your new role 'til it becomes second nature. If you're in a hotel and you think someone's paying you attention, the last thing you do is react. Suppose it's a former squaddie and he's looking at you, pay no attention. He'll think, 'No, it can't be.' Never panic.

CAROLINE: I don't think Jack was ever the same again... it affected his nerves...little things, you know, in the garden, anything sudden...and me.

I.R.A.: One of the first things I did when I got to a new city was find the big department store...anywhere with a side-door or a back-door, so you can lose a tail. It means you've always got a plan in your head. I had an idea I was being followed in Birmingham one day. My best store for losing people was in Manchester. Got on a train to Manchester, used my store, lost my tail.

CAROLINE: We were having a good conference, except on the drive down; I shall never forget it, it was pelting with rain. We had to take our best bibs and tuckers; I was in a dreadful hurry as usual, I didn't have time to pack properly; I got out of the car in front of the hotel armed with a lot of things on coat-hangers...there were the assembled cameras of the press...and I dropped half the things I was carrying in the mud.

I.R.A.: It wasn't any one individual that bombed Brighton; it was the organisation.

CAROLINE: Thursday…it was the usual conference agenda…we finished about five thirty, followed I suppose by the inevitable cocktail party. I would have been in a very dressy dress. Then we went out to dinner.

I.R.A.: I'd booked into the room three and a half weeks previously.

CAROLINE: We went to a very expensive, very nice French restaurant in Brighton, the Caprice…we went with six or eight friends…Norman and Margaret Tebbit, John Wakeham and his wife were there…well-known people. It was a lovely evening considering it was early October…a lovely evening, not at all cold. It really was a very good restaurant, and it was a fun evening, you know…we were all good friends. I remember looking round the table and seeing all those smiling faces. Six hours later half of them were dead.

I.R.A.: I used a standard video recorder.

CAROLINE: We went back to the hotel, we had a drink in the bar…this must have been about one o'clock in the morning.

I.R.A.: The mechanism had to be as simple as possible.

CAROLINE: One of our party, Eric Taylor, had to ring his constituency in Lancashire…one of his members had gone to a Conservative ball and died, and Eric had to ring the family to say what had happened.

I.R.A.: A safety circuit…a main circuit…I set the timer…

CAROLINE: The bar was on the ground floor. There were ten or twelve of us chatting…it probably wasn't about politics at all. Do you know, I think we were on the third floor…I'm sure we were.

I.R.A.: Twenty-six days, six hours and thirty-six minutes

CAROLINE: We went up in the lift about two...two fifteen...about that...we went to bed.

I.R.A.: I put it behind the bath panelling.

CAROLINE: Three...quarter past three...I don't think we really realised what had happened until the chimney came down, and took our bathroom with it. There was a hole where the bathroom was...I don't like to think...I suppose it was ten feet from the bed...I suppose we were on the edge. Jack said, 'It's a bomb.' I always remember him saying, 'It's a bomb.' We were in the most crucial bit really. We got out of bed...people were shouting, 'Get out, get out'...there was glass everywhere...shredded curtains and things...people shouting, 'Come this way, come this way.' There was emergency lighting, nothing else. I found a dress on a chair, put that on. Jack had left his suit on the end of the bed. He put it on on top of his pyjamas. He picked up his shoes and socks...I picked up a pair of boots and two anoraks...in fact, Jack grumbled because I was halfway out the door and went back to pick them up. When we got outside there was an old man in just his pyjamas, so I gave him one of the anoraks. Jack gave his socks to somebody. We went out through an emergency door onto a fire-escape. There was no panic; everyone was very calm.

Enter S.S.2.

CAROLINE: We knew straight away people hadn't come out. There was a column, you see...definitely a column which came down. Under our room was Anthony Berry and his wife...you see, he was killed and she wasn't.

I.R.A.: Sixteen years later I met Jo Berry. Her father had been killed. We sat down and talked. It was an intense experience.

CAROLINE: John Wakeham was in the room next to us… below him were Norman and Margaret Tebbit.

S.S.2: I was drifting in and out of consciousness…we were able to talk to each other…and, of course, because I was next to my wife, I was aware that she was gradually becoming paralysed. The most disconcerting thing…the debris was holding my head in a vice, and every time the wreckage moved, it twisted my head a bit more. If it had shifted seriously, it would have ripped my head off. I was wound up in the bedding; the dust was choking me. I knew I was bleeding badly…I lost the top of my hip, and I had a great gouge out of my belly.

CAROLINE: Everyone was very quiet out on the seafront.

S.S.2: We lay there for four hours in pitch darkness.

CAROLINE: We messed about on the street until M & S opened and we were all told to go and get something to wear. We were in a daze… M & S is not a shop I'm used to anyway. I forgot to buy makeup…I didn't realise they sold it even.

S.S.2: I don't remember much.

CAROLINE: Everyone had to be on the platform at nine. Margaret Thatcher had said the conference would start as usual. The taxi people took us to the conference centre for nothing, which was good of them.

I.R.A.: Of course I regret the suffering I caused but circumstances made our actions inevitable.

CAROLINE: It wasn't until the Saturday that the police said there was a possibility we might get our stuff out of the hotel. They were looking for a body, you see…this woman…they couldn't find her…she'd gone to the toilet in the room where the bomb was…they say it was when she turned the light on, but I don't think it was…she went into the bathroom, and the force of the explosion blew her right to the back of the hotel somewhere.

I.R.A.: You have to put events into a historical perspective. I would say we didn't have any recourse other than engage in that armed struggle.

S.S.2: And I would say, 'This is for you my friend,' and let him have it from close range.

CAROLINE: The man who put the bomb there...he killed my friends and he can't bring them back, which is so awful. He should spend the rest of his life in prison, and not in a luxy place either...half these prisons are like first class hotels.

S.S.2: Forgiveness isn't overrated, but there has to be regret, and there has to be a determination to make amends for what you've done. If he were doing that I could find it in my heart to forgive him.

I.R.A.: Sitting here now...it's like talking about someone else.

CAROLINE: The year after...no, not the year after, the year after that, the conference was held in Brighton again. Jack and I were put in the room where the bomb went off. Not the most sensitive thing in the world, but you just have to sort of...well, you have to be there.

Burst of birdsong from an English woodland garden.

S.S.2: (*In bare feet.*) We've got nuthatches, woodpeckers, all the tits, wrens, there's one of my robin friends look... we give them a bit of help at this time of year...not all the year round, but when it's cold like this. We also get the pheasants...they're asylum seekers...we allow them asylum in the garden. Mind you, I belong to a shoot a few miles down the road and if I catch them there...

I'm sorry…I haven't got round to getting properly
dressed. I'm afraid we're in a bit of a bugger's muddle
this morning. Our new carer, it's her first morning…so
we have to go through the whole routine step by step.
I've got to go and do my second little task…I'll be back
down in a minute…

S.S.2 exits as U.V.F. comes on.

I.R.A.: I was arrested in Glasgow. The Special Branch men
said, 'Pat, there are police forces queuing up to talk to
you.' I was sentenced to multiple life. My dad came to
see me once but he was turned away because he didn't
have proper identification. That's the last time I saw
him.

U.V.F.: When I was in Longkesh, I ended up with
an honours degree from the Open University in
Mathematics and Computers and Systems; in actual
fact, it was the only subject that I was any good at, but
like so many young men in Belfast at that time I had left
school at fifteen.

I.R.A.: I got two degrees…one in Modern Literature and
Art, and one in Politics. I took as my subject 'The
Misrepresentation of the Conflict in Popular Fiction'.
And I got a doctorate.

U.V.F.: I saw this other man sitting there in the library…a
Republican. I knew exactly who he was; I knew exactly
what he'd done. As the morning wore on, I fancied
a wee cup of tea; but then I thought it would be very
rude to make one for me and not for him. 'No, fuck it,'
I thought, 'I won't,'…but then I found myself saying,
'Would you like a wee cup of tea?'

I.R.A.: Yes I would, thank you.

U.V.F.: We both talked…we developed a tremendous
friendship. We were both working-class men from

Belfast; we had both put cardboard into our shoes when it rained; by and large, I could have lived his life.

I.R.A.: And he mine.

S.S.2 re-enters.

S.S.2: There, I've put some slippers on. I suppose it was rather an elaborate way to prove I don't have cloven hooves. Mo Mowlam called me into her office...she said, 'I'm going to release him later this week...I didn't want you finding out from the television.' I said, 'Thank you for telling me.' She said, 'You don't seem upset.' I said, 'There's no point; but tell me something...if I'm waiting for him at the gates and I give him both barrels of my twelve-bore, is that murder? Or is it good housekeeping?' She said, 'You wouldn't.' I said, 'Mo, I would, but for one fact, and that is the problem it would cause my wife.'

The CARER knocks at the door.

S.S.2: Yes?

CARER: My lord...your wife wants to get into the little chair.

S.S.2: The big chair?

CARER: No, the little chair.

S.S.2: She wants to get into the little chair. Right, I'll come.

The CARER and S.S.2 go.

I.R.A.: When I got out I remember seeing the trees from the prison van. I'd forgotten what a tree looked like.

U.V.F.: No, it did not achieve the goal that I desired. If anything I contributed to the expansion of the I.R.A. by violently attacking it. I know that now.

I.R.A.: I'd love to merge quietly into the background, but…
you see over the road there…those pubs…The Crown,
Robinson's…they're loyalist pubs…I might have a bit of
trouble if I tried to go in there. It's going to be like that
for a long time to come.

U.V.F.: I now work in Post Traumatic Stress Syndrome.
People who kill someone else also kill part of
themselves. They lose part of their humanity.

I.R.A.: Very difficult…very difficult to live with some of the
things that happened.

I.R.A. and U.V.F. go together. Enter S.S.2

S.S.2: After Ian Gow was murdered, I was warned there
was an active I.R.A. hit squad looking for a soft target…
told me to be careful. Helpful remark. So I went to
sleep with a twelve-bore under the bed, loaded with a
couple of heavy cartridges. Three a.m. I say to my wife,
'There's someone out on the drive.' She listened…she
said, 'You're right.' I picked up the gun, slid out the side
door…I'm in my dressing-gown and slippers…I looked
up the drive…there's one bloke by the Range Rover
and I can see the legs of another guy who's on the far
side of the car. I was the happiest man in the world.
A twelve-bore's gonna take out anyone with a hand
gun. I moved along in the shadows…and then, as in all
good training, identify the target…it's a police officer…
checking the Range Rover, checking it was clean…
didn't want to disturb us unduly. I was so disappointed.
They talk of a left and right of snipe or woodcock…
but a left and right of I.R.A., now that would have been
something. I'm afraid Terrorism makes you like that. My
belief is you have to be ruthless about killing the guys
at the sharp end and do some extremely deep thinking
about taking away the base that sustains them…you
can't, you won't succeed without doing both. Here's my
wife.

The CARER wheels his wife into the room in 'the small chair'.

WIFE: Right in please…no further, further, now round… and now back…no, no, no, on the rug…on the back rug…there, thank you.

CARER: I go prepare the lunch now.

WIFE: Yes, thank you.

S.S.2: Thank you.

The CARER goes.

S.S.2: The I.R.A. hit-list starts with the Queen and goes down from there. The amount of protection depends where you are on the list and whether you're going up or down.

WIFE: A bit like 'Popular Classics' on Classic F.M.

S.S.2: We've been in some strange situations, especially in Northern Ireland…

WIFE: Robert and Nora…

S.S.2: He was a tee-totaller.

WIFE: Oh you've spoiled the story now. We'd had a long day, we get back, settle down on the sofa, Nora turned to me, 'Will you have a drink?' I said, 'Yes, please.' She said, 'Would you like an Ovaltine?' I said to Norman later I was dying for a G and T.

S.S.2: Robert said to me, 'We've put you in the front bedroom…it's a bit noisy, I'm afraid, with the traffic…I hope you don't mind…but that's the one with the bullet-proof glass.' It was like being in a B-movie only I didn't care for the scriptwriter. But the security chaps who looked after me…

WIFE: Marvellous…wonderful men.

S.S.2: One of my chaps I still see very regularly…he comes down here every year.

WIFE: He takes me to the Chelsea Flower Show.

S.S.2: Some people hang on to their security. You mustn't say this, but Ted Heath still has a driver. I don't know why. Who would want to kill Ted Heath? Nobody I can think of, except possibly Mrs Thatcher.

WIFE: They become part of your life.

S.S.2: One of the things that has made modern society so vulnerable is the speed at which people can get around the world. The mad Mahdi may have killed Gordon at Khartoum, but he was no threat at all to the man on the Peckham omnibus. And then you have to look at the reasons why there's so much anger in the Muslim world. I always liken it…it's the rage of Caliban. In the fifteenth century the Muslim world and Christendom were even pegging, but nothing of importance has come out of the Muslim world in the last five hundred years. Somehow they've been screwed. If you're a terrorist, you have to use a western gun, western telephone, even western explosives. They've been left picking up the crumbs. And it's certainly not a lack of ability.

My wife and I were in hospital that Christmas…actually I escaped just before Christmas…

WIFE: Surprise, surprise.

S.S.2: I stayed at Chequers, but I joined my wife for Christmas lunch at Stoke Mandeville, in the spinal unit, and the surgeons arrived with a carving knife and fork, and a turkey on a trolley…they were going to do it properly.

WIFE: There were three or four of them.

S.S.2: Yes, there was a Jew, a Palestinian, an Egyptian, and I can't remember the other one...not a Christian among them...they all got on extremely well. When we liberate them, they flourish. If we don't, there's this huge frustration...it can't be my fault, it's not Allah, so it must be the Infidels.

WIFE: I was in Stoke Mandeville for a year and Stanmore for a year. In the spinal units there was a lot of laughter...I couldn't be miserable for long...you need each other...especially when they say you'll never walk again; and things like not being able to hug your grandchildren. But if you have a happy marriage... Can I go now? It must be nearly lunchtime.

S.S.2: Ingrid!

WIFE: The biggest problem is getting carers...getting girls in their twenties to commit for six months minimum, hopefully longer.

S.S.2: Very difficult.

WIFE: Very difficult. Still, this one wants to stay for two years.

S.S.2: I shall clasp her to me.

CARER: (*Knocking.*) My lord?

S.S.2: Yes, my wife would like to go to the kitchen.

Undoes the wheelbrake.

There you go. Steady as we go. That's it.

Ingrid wheels wife out.

Enter ENVOY, PHOEBE and AMB..

PHOEBE: It's such a luxury to be able to leave. A couple of times something has happened to delay a departure, or things have started to get messy, and you get an inkling of what it must be like to be trapped there.

AMB.: I've got to have heart surgery as a result of the pulmonary emboli. They said I've got three years to live tops, but recently the doctors are more hopeful.

PHOEBE: Then you get away, and get on the plane and have a gin. You leave it all behind. You move on to the next thing...for me it's been the Tsunami.

AMB.: I'm off to Blackburn. I couldn't be in more trouble if I tried, but in for a penny... I'm standing against Jack Straw at the General Election in his Blackburn constituency. I'm standing on a human rights ticket... 'A vote for Jack Straw is a vote for torture'.

PHOEBE: One experience stays with me. I was in Congo, the situation was a mess, lots of separated children, some found amongst piles of bodies and so on. One day, a rebel group started firing near where we were working. We all had to run and lost some of the children, and eventually we were forced out of the area. I realised that in the chaos I had lost my bag which had my passport *et cetera* in it. Later that day, one of our local staff...a young man...turned up with my bag. He'd gone back and picked it up. One of the rebels had beaten him up, but he got away with it and brought it back for me. Why would he do that?

We talked to all the staff and said we didn't expect them to go back to work the next day, and since I was feeling...well, yes, I was feeling distinctly nervous...I was hoping they would say they didn't want to. But they didn't even consider not carrying on; so we did.

ENVOY: I've talked about the simplicity of faith, which I do believe in; I could say in the face of my captors, 'You've tried to break my body...you haven't; you've tried to break my mind...you haven't...but my soul is not yours to possess.' But that in essence is exactly what is being said by them… 'You can invade my country, do what you will, but my soul is not yours to possess.'

PHOEBE: I will never forget the spirit of those people. They worked for months rescuing children. They went up rivers in canoes and walked for days through impenetrable bush, sometimes being attacked and harassed. They were well-educated, many had university degrees, but had to live, by accident of birth, in a country with one of the most corrupt governments, in chronic conflict and poverty…yet they just got on with it.

Enter S.S.1., P.K.K., N.R.A. and A.A.B.

S.S.2: Nobody's pretending we're perfect…we're never going to be a hundred per cent correct and honest; but liberal states have enough to make them worth defending.

N.R.A.: Even if I'm dying, I could remember the day I came to Denmark. My first mother and father is Denmark. To cry and to feel is given me by Denmark. In Africa I wanted a damn gun, and I could kill the lot of them. In Denmark I've wished for not even a small knife.

P.K.K.: I believe I'm strong mentally, otherwise I don't last twenty-one years in jail; but I understand I am not always behaving rationally.

N.R.A.: As a child I saw what a grown-up would expect to see only a glimpse of once in their lifetime. An old person grew in me like wildfire. I'm twenty-eight years old now; sometimes I feel fifteen, sometimes I'm two hundred.

P.K.K.: I get anger about stupid things…for instance if someone throws litter in the street. Order…there has to be order. I have to have a mental plan to survive, day by day by day by day.

N.R.A.: I wish I had the trust and confidence to love an African man, but the others took away my trust for all of them. The question of marrying an African man is out. The ones I've known made me look at the rest in the wrong way. I'm a very new person...the old person is walking away...I'm staying. I wanted to hate my father, but now I want to think how to love him.

Exit.

S.S.1: I split the movement. I split Sinn Fein from the I.R.A...I did that.

S.S.2: If you have the responsibility of protecting people, you have to be ruthless. If there are things you could have done and didn't, what do you say to yourself when you wake at three in the morning and stare at the ceiling for the rest of your life?

S.S.1: I miss my constituency...I liked the people...you could have a proper conversation. I do lecture tours now, and I've got my knitting. I'm doing a bedspread. I enjoy talking to young people...you feel you might just get somewhere.

PHOEBE: Of course so much of it makes you despair, and makes you afraid, for yourself and for humanity, I suppose. But then you sit on the floor, and play with a kid who tells you horrors worse than any nightmare, and yet there he is, sitting there and playing, and behaving perfectly normally to all intents and purposes. Yes, you can absolutely see hope in individuals... enormously... Yes, if I had to say, that would be it.

A.A.B.: Let me tell you something, my friend. Everything good inside me is dead. I will probably never see my wife and children...one child I've never even seen born.

Can I have a cigarette here? No?

P.K.K.: Now for the good news. I live in Tottenham. I married a woman called Birsel a year ago and we have a three-month-old daughter called Dijle…it's the name of a river in Kurdestan…it's name means 'The River that gives Life'. So, it doesn't succeed…all the torture… my balls still work. They couldn't beat me in that respect.

A.A.B.: Fun? You think I can have fun? How can I have fun? But I will ask you this also. How can you judge me unless you have lived the life I have lived? Do you want me to think logically like you, my British friends… you, who gave my country to the Israeli…you who are behind all the trouble in Ireland…all the trouble in South Africa…all the trouble in India? What do you know of hopelessness and despair? I must have a cigarette. I'm going out.

Enter BETHLEHEM SCHOOLGIRL with her homework.

PHOEBE: This has all just spilled out of my head really… nothing terribly edifying or original, or with any particular meaning, but I thought I'd tell it to you anyway, since you seemed interested.

P.K.K.: I never told my story, not before. I'm pleased to tell it. Thank you for listening. Reality cannot hide forever. You might as well try and cover the sun with mud.

GIRL: This year things are getting worse. Last April… the saddest day; one of the girls in the form below me, Christine, was killed by an Israeli sniper. The Israelis said it was a mistake, but they can't bring her back, can they?

When I first saw the Twin Towers on television, I felt sorry. But now I feel happy that they died. It's their turn to suffer. I could see many thousands of them die. I wouldn't feel a thing.

RESOURCE
MATERIAL

Alecky Blythe
...on verbatim theatre

The technique I use to create verbatim plays reproduces on stage moments from everyday life that I could never write, giving a voice to characters that are rarely heard in the theatre. I create plays from recorded interviews which are edited but not transcribed. Rather than learning a text, the actors copy the speech patterns and physicality of the interviewee. The show is rehearsed and performed with the actors wearing earphones through which they hear the edited interview playing, and they copy exactly what they hear, including every cough, stutter and hesitation. By keeping the earphones on during the performance the chance of the actors slipping into their own speech pattern or parody is limited because they have to keep up with what they are listening to.

Come Out Eli; photo by Ian Cole

This technique was taught at the Actors Centre by Mark Wing-Davey who inspired me to make my first show *Come Out Eli.* The original idea had been to make a show about fear, so a gun-siege seemed a good starting point. But as our work progressed I realized a story was unfolding that I was lucky to have been documenting from the beginning. Unlike a traditional playwright who has complete control of the plot and characters, a verbatim writer has little control over where the story might go, and this is what is so exciting and enlightening about the form. The most surprising twist in this story came when I contacted a traumatized hostage. His interview took the narrative in a most unexpected direction: he wanted either a sexual or financial reward for his story, neither of which I was willing to give him. I had not found the pathos I was looking for but something far more revealing instead.

The material collected at the siege was immediately interesting. People were less intimidated by the microphone than I had found in more formal interview situations because they were engaged in the drama occurring in their immediate environment and this freed them up to talk so spontaneously. I try to be as casual as possible so that people do not feel as if they are on the spot or under any pressure to come up with anything witty or intelligent. Prepared anecdotes are not what I'm interested in. I try to make the microphone as unobtrusive as possible. There is a fine line between getting it close enough to the subject to pick up everything that they are saying and constantly reminding them that they are being recorded and making them self-conscious.

In order to encourage people to open up about their lives, I often have to open up about mine in order to gain their trust. In *A Man In A Box Part II* I meet a drunk who turns the interview around and forces me to confess things about myself which I had not previously had the courage to admit to anyone. I became the subject without even realising it. Often the richest material has come out of situations that I would rather not be in, but the microphone gives me license to ask things that I otherwise would not. I found myself in a very uncomfortable situation making *Cruising* (which is about pensioners looking for love) when Maureen – the lead character – interrogated her friend Margaret and recent fiancé Geoff about their decision to marry. There were moments

during the interview between the three of them when I just wanted to say something to ease the tension in the room, but I had to stop myself from intervening as I knew these would be powerful moments on stage.

Cruising: photo by Ian Cole

In the edit I try to distill the characters and the key moments for dramatic effect. This is where you can control the story by being selective over what parts of the interview to present. Hours of recording are condensed into one hour (the usual length of my shows) so the characters and the action are heightened to a certain extent. However, the technique allows actors to perform extensively edited versions of the interviews without slipping into caricature as they are constantly reminded of the real interviewee through their earphones. Of course the actors are not just mouth-pieces and their interpretations inevitably colour the portrayal, but I think this technique keeps it to a minimum.

The intimacy of the interview makes the audience feel as if the characters are talking to them directly, and the relationship I had with the interviewee is that which the audience experiences. However, the fact that these private moments have been transported into a public arena is what makes them all the more surprising, especially as they are re-enacted with the uncanny immediacy that the technique produces. The way people communicate in real life is far more absurd and inarticulate than we realise if we take the time to stop and listen to it.

Alecky Blythe
Artistic Director, Recorded Delivery.

Come Out Eli was created from interviews conducted during the Hackney Seige in 2002. *A Man in a Box Part II* was created from interviews conducted at David Blaine's stunt in a glass box at Tower Bridge in 2003; and *Cruising*, from interviews with pensioners.

Peter Cheeseman
...on documentary theatre

When I started my thirty-seven year stint as Director of the Victoria Theatre in Stoke-on-Trent I had no notion that documentary theatre would become such a prominent part of its repertoire and its reputation. I had been given the job by Stephen Joseph. He had set up a small touring company to stage new plays and explore the potential of theatre in the round. When he decided to forsake active participation with the company, he generously passed on to me the artistic independence he had always enjoyed from his Board. I had the freedom and the responsibility to create the programme and to make ends meet.

Reflecting Stephen's priorities, half our output was new work, and the rest contemporary plays of distinction and major classics. I believed strongly that the first necessity for winning an audience was to stay put. Touring dissipated the support it built up in any visit because of the gap before the next. It also leached resources of energy as well as cash. I wanted to explore a relationship with one coherent community to make the theatre at home there in its battered landscape. The theatre documentaries owe their origin as well as their particular style and choice of subject matter to these circumstances.

I was inspired by *Oh What A Lovely War!* at Theatre Workshop and longed to emulate Joan Littlewood. I felt it was important to cement our relationship with North Staffordshire people by telling the stories of their trials and achievements. No other agency was providing this kind of food for their self-respect. I never believed that a theatre performance was likely to make somebody change their vote. But I do think that we can help to create a positive social environment and a higher level of self-regard for the members of a community making it more likely that they will vote at all.

As time passed and experience accumulated, I tried to make the creation of a documentary on a local subject function as a combination of a community festival and a real creative workshop. The process involved the participation of all the acting company and almost all the staff in one way or another. It soon endorsed the spirit of ensemble nurtured by our policy of long term actors' contracts and a repertoire system of programming. It began to act as a test-bed for new styles of performance, welcomed by our associated writers such as Peter Terson , Shane Connaughton and Ken Campbell.

One element in the assembly of the documentary is fundamental to the working blueprint we developed: only primary source material was to be included. It was not to be written, but assembled only from the actual records and observations of the participants and observers of the real events. For the first two we made some scenes from improvisation or devising. But it completely invalidated the authority of a narrative composed of the actual records. So we phased this out by the third production.

The first was *The Jolly Potters* in 1964 to end our second season. It was an account of the social miseries of the mid 19th Century and of the Chartist Riots of 1842 which brought all the industrial districts of the country to a standstill. There was plenty of printed and verbatim evidence and it was lively stuff. But though we were all keen, it was a very alarming experience. But we made it, and it worked.

The second, *The Staffordshire Rebels* in 1965 dealt with the involvement of Staffordshire people in the English

Civil Wars. We nearly had a catastrophe: too much material; too little time to dramatise it. The only thing that kept our spirits up was the fact that the BBC filmed all our terrifying struggles. We

only flagged when they switched off the bright lights and went off for a break. But the music of the time and the challenge of staging the battles and the King's execution were a delight. They worked and once again proved the power of acting and the strength of theatre in the round.

By the time of the third play I had learned enough to plan the whole process and identify the style that was emerging. It was to be performed in two parts, musical scenes alternating with spoken scenes throughout. Songs were often used to convey simple information and were exempt from the primary source rule. If we could find authentic songs of the time then we used them, but this didn't happen very often. I did the initial research, aided by the resident dramatist or an actor/writer, and as time went by the acting company were brought in to help structure the research into possible scenes which would be filled out in rehearsal .The whole process took about six months.

This third play was *The Knotty* (1966) about the life and death of our local railway company. It was the first to use the outcome of recorded interviews, in this case of the now elderly railway men who had worked on the line as boys. This development was inspired by our friendship with two major documentary directors from the BBC: Philip Donnellan in film and the radio revolutionary Charles Parker. This led us to a reservoir of creativity. 'Listen,' said Charles Parker. 'Listen to people talking.' And I found what I had sought for a long time: the muscular strength and unselfconscious flashes of imagery that characterise vernacular speech.

Tape-recorded dialogue formed a part of every succeeding documentary. In the historic accounts of the lives of

Josiah Wedgwood and of Hugh Bourne, founder of primitive Methodism, it provided a modern comment on the historic action. The other five were entirely composed from the oral material: *Hands Up! For you the War is Ended* (1971) from British POWs; *Fight for Shelton Bar!* (1974) from steelworkers; *Miner Dig the Coal* (1981) from coalminers. Our first in the New Theatre was *The Dirty Hill* (1990) and supported the campaign to prevent the open-cast mining of a hilltop in the middle of the city. The residents affected – Councillors, miners, environmentalists, archaeologists and British Coal officials – were all contributors to this one. Our last documentary *Nice Girls* (1993) recorded the adventures of four brave miner's wives who tried to save one of our last two working pits from closure by occupying it. They failed.

The most interesting feature of the kind of documentary theatre we developed was that adhering to the primary source rule compelled us to develop all kinds of stylistic solutions to include essential, but seemingly unperformable, elements in the story when we had no suitable contemporary accounts. The most memorable were from *The Jolly Potters* and *The Knotty*. The first was simply four actors miming an imagined cup-making machine, the great dread of the working potters. The second was a poker-faced dance of half a dozen surveyors' polemen representing the battles of twenty-four railway companies who tried to get the local railway contract. As the finished cup flew out of the machine and at the amazing ending of the railway battles there was that most satisfying sound to be heard in a theatre – a great peal of laughter leading straight into an extended roar of applause.

Peter Cheeseman
Theatre Director, old and New Victoria theatre, North Staffordshire (1962 – 1998)

Elyse Dodgson
...on personal testimony

I became interested in using personal testimony to make theatre when I was a drama teacher in the late 1970s. Vauxhall Manor in South London was an inner-city girls' comprehensive school where over 80% of the girls came from an Afro- Caribbean background. Over a period of five years, girls aged 11–18 used research and testimony to create theatre that explored social and historical issues that were important to them. The subjects they chose were often directly related to their experiences of being female and black. From 1981-1982 we created *Motherland,* based upon the personal testimony of twenty-three women in the local community who came to Britain from the West Indies in the 1950s. The women shared their life stories with us; most of them were the mothers of the girls involved in the play. The girls recorded interviews with their own mothers and then reached out to neighbours and friends. They transcribed their tapes and used the testimony to inspire their own writing. *Motherland* was first performed at the Oval House Theatre in July 1982.

Motherland, 1982

At the Royal Court for almost twenty years now, I continue to be inspired by this method of creating theatre – a method that can tackle big important subjects and also be a tool for young playwrights. The young women involved in *Motherland* often spoke about how taking part in verbatim theatre helped them to discover things even they didn't know. Playwrights may be inspired by their own experience and imagination but in between there are the things they need to research and discover. Getting out the tape recorder and listening to the fingerprints of individual voices can be a breakthrough for writers learning about character and dialogue.

The International Department at the Royal Court has had the opportunity to introduce verbatim techniques in many places. In Kampala, Uganda the group interviewed women in prison, many of whom committed crimes against their co-wives. In Bethlehem we gathered check-point stories as people were asked to talk about their experiences of crossing from the West Bank into Jerusalem and back again. In Salvador, Brazil a group of very young writers gathered testimony describing a particular day in the past year when the police went on strike. In every case the finished plays examined worlds in great detail, worlds we know little about.

However, nothing prepared me for the impact that this method of working would have in post-perestroika Russia. Asked to do a three-day seminar in Moscow in the autumn of 1999, the group chose to focus on ethnic discrimination and investigated the story of one of the participants who was from Abkhazia and had lost her lover in the war with Georgia. The idea of exploring a contemporary subject first-hand through interviews in the field was something that had not been attempted by many of the artists before and the excitement spread. I returned in April 2000 with directors Stephen

Moscow Open City Moscow 1999, developed in collaboration with the Royal Court.

Daldry and James Macdonald who helped to set up a project based on interviews with the homeless in Moscow Central Station. After that, the whole country was conducting verbatim projects: with coalminers in Kemerovo, soldiers who were wounded in Chechnya, drug addicts in Irkutsk, with those affected by the Kursk submarine tragedy in Murmansk, and with the Nenet hunters of the Yamal Tundra region.

Many of these projects led to plays that were completely made up of verbatim testimony while others inspired original work like Vassily Sigarev's early play *The Pit* which explores the world of a small Russian town where narcotics, AIDS and prison life exist in close proximity.

Alive from Palestine 2001photo provided by Al Kasaba Theatre; photo by Michael J O'Brien

In recent years at the Royal Court it has been a great privilege to be associated with the development and the production of international plays like *Waiting Room Germany* (1995) by Klaus Pohl about the responses of East and West Germans five years after the Wall came down; *Via Dolorosa* (1998) by David Hare about his own unique journey to Israel and Palestine; and *Alive From Palestine* (2001) by Al-Kasaba Theatre, Ramallah, subtitled 'Stories under Occupation'. All of these authors used the verbatim method very differently but have produced challenging, provocative theatre and rare insights into many diverse subjects. They are instructive in the best sense of the word.

Elyse Dodgson
Associate Director International, Royal Court Theatre

David Hare
...on factual theatre

In a famous letter to the novelist F. Scott Fitzgerald, Ernest Hemingway expressed reservations about his friend's great masterpiece *Tender Is the Night*. Scott, Hemingway said, had taken elements of his own relationship with his wife Zelda, he had added in events which had befallen their mutual friends, Gerald and Sara Murphy, and then he had laid on top of this factual mélange a third layer, this time of pure invention. This was, Hemingway said, no way to write, because the reader was distracted by the question of what was real and what was not. In his reply, Fitzgerald pointed out that this was, actually, one of the means by which writers of fiction had always operated. Elizabethan dramatists, including Shakespeare, had regarded it as normal artfully to mix facts about people who had really existed with what these same people inspired in the author's imagination. Hemingway had the perfect right to doubt Scott's success with what he called 'composite characters'. What he had no right to do was question the method itself.

Bella Merlin, Lloyd Hutchinson and Flaminia Cinque in *The Permanent Way* by David Hare, 1993; photo by John Haynes

It has also long been standard practice for certain playwrights to choose to make their plays out of real-life dialogue. For myself, I've been involved, as producer or writer, in such projects for over thirty years, thinking the method no stranger than that of a sculptor who prefers to work from rusting iron abandoned on a waste-tip than from self-cast plaster or concrete. Never for a moment has it occurred to me that such works, using verbatim dialogue, organized, arranged and orchestrated with proper thematic care should involve less labour, skill or creative imagination than those dreamt up in the privacy of a study. And yet recently those of us who have sometimes written by this method have had to confront a couple of complaints: first, it has been said that plays based on real-life dialogue are somehow not 'real' plays. And second, that they are merely part of a wave of fashion blowing through British theatre, which will soon, like everything, blow itself out.

It's as hard for most of us to take such objections seriously as it was for Fitzgerald to write back to his obviously jealous friend. All revolutions in art, said someone, are a return to realism. Given that most art-forms, in the hands of metropolitan elites, tend to drift away from reality, what could be more bracing or healthy than occasionally to offer authentic news of overlooked thought and feeling? Isn't it the noblest function of democracy to give a voice to a voiceless? And where better than in a medium whose genius is for sustaining scrutiny? What a welcome corrective to the cosy art-for-art's-sake racket which theatre all too easily becomes!

And how, possibly, can the current excellence of verbatim work be dismissed purely as part of a vogue? Documentary theatre, like physical theatre or classical theatre or children's theatre, has become altogether too broad and invigorating a stream to be treated as a passing phenomenon, or, silliest of all, as something with a single, common character. Any fair-minded observer will immediately remark on its variety. There are good and bad documentary plays, as there are of any kind. How can you make a sensible comparison between the formal tribunal plays in which the Tricycle Theatre has specialised – like the *Stephen Lawrence Inquiry* – and more free-wheeling pieces like *Come Out Eli,* the Arcola's re-creation of a Hackney siege, with the author herself being propositioned by another of the characters? What purpose is served by inventing some sort of generic dumping-ground for anything based on real events and people (*Democracy,* anyone? *Copenhagen?*) and then pretending that, if you do, any two plays work to the same rules?

No, what we are witnessing is one of those moments at which theatre excels. Once again, the art-form is looking outside itself – and more profitably than any other – to try and expose the way in which we all, as individuals, are or are not connected to the great events of history. Yes, *Electra* seems timely. But so does the idea of *Talking to Terrorists.* Good theatre works by reflection *and* by representation. Why can't we just admit that theatre using real people has become a fabulously rich and varied strand which, for many years, has been pumping red cells into the dramatic bloodstream? And if this kind of work does appear even more necessary and affecting at this particular time, doesn't that tell us something about the time as much as the work?

The Colour of Justice by Richard Norton Taylor, Tricycle Theatre 1999, photo by John Haynes

David Hare
Playwright